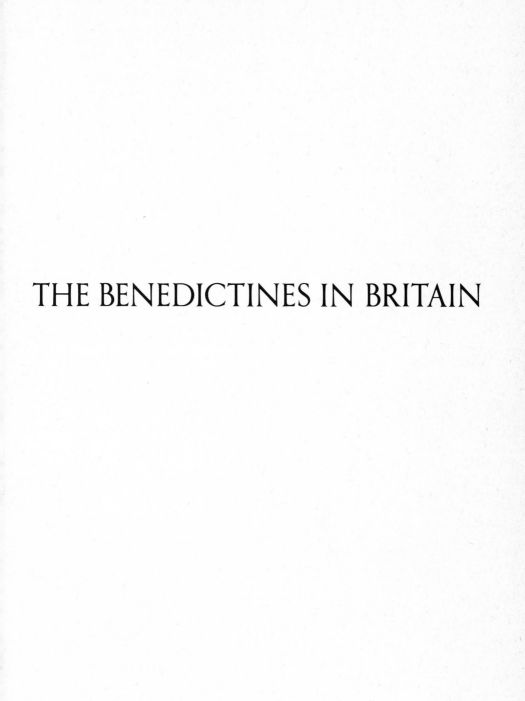

THE BENEDICTINES IN BRITAIN

British Library Series No. 3

THE
BENEDICTINES
IN BRITAIN

THE BRITISH LIBRARY

©1980 The British Library
ISBN 0 904654 47 8
Published by the British Library
Reference Division Publications,
Great Russell Street
London WC1B 3DG

British Library Cataloguing in Publication Data

British Library
  The Benedictines in Britain — (British Library. Series; 3)
  1. British Library. Department of Manuscripts — Catalogs
  2. Benedictines in Great Britain — Manuscripts — Catalogs
  3. Manuscripts, English — England — London — Exhibitions
  I. Title   II. Turner, Derek Howard   III. Series
  016.271′1′041   Z6621.B84

Designed by Frank Phillips
Set in 12/13pt Bembo by
Channel Eight Ltd, Bexhill-on-Sea
Printed in Great Britain by
Staples Printing Group Ltd
at Rochester, Kent

Cover:
*The Golden Book of St Albans, John
Whethamstede, abbot of St Albans 1420–
1440 and 1451–1465.*

CONTENTS

Throughout the text, 'exhibits' are referred to by number. These are the exhibits in the British Library's exhibition 'The Benedictines in Britain', 11th July–30th November 1980. Unless more explicitly stated they are in the Department of Manuscripts, the Reference Division, the British Library. A complete list of exhibits is given at the end of the book. Bold figures in square brackets refer to pictures in this book.

LIST OF
ILLUSTRATIONS

FOREWORD

The year 1980 is being celebrated throughout the world as the fifteen-hundredth anniversary of the birth of St Benedict, whose rule has been the leading inspiration for monastic life in the western church. Those who vow themselves to it are called Benedictines and once staffed places like Westminster Abbey, Canterbury Cathedral, and Durham Cathedral, to mention only three ecclesiastical establishments famed in Britain's story. Western civilization owes its life-blood to monks and nuns. In the early Middle Ages monasteries were the centres of civilization in western Europe. Since then, down to the present day, their contribution to progress, everywhere, has been far from negligible. Monks and nuns leave the world in order to find God. In finding him they find they have much to give to the world, in missionary work, in education, in craftsmanship, and many other fields.

Benedictines have always been associated with the making of books, as authors, copyists, and decorators. In recognition of an incalculable debt to the Benedictines and their books, the British Library is publishing the present volume, in conjunction with an exhibition of the same title held in the King's Library from 11th July to 30th November 1980. Both the exhibition and the publication aim to give a picture of Benedictine life and achievement in Britain, principally through manuscript books of Benedictine origin from the Middle Ages. The post-Reformation period has not been neglected, however. The books in the exhibition, which are also described in this study, range from plain texts to elaborate works of art and while most are from the Library's collections, some have been generously lent from outside.

The British Library wishes to express sincere gratitude to the following institutions who have lent to the exhibition: Downside Abbey, Bath (exhibits 121, 122, 124, 125, 127); Nashdom Abbey, Burnham (exhibit 120); Prinknash Abbey, Gloucester (exhibits 31 and 128); the British Museum, London, Department of Medieval and Later Antiquities (exhibits 72–79); Lambeth Palace Library, London (exhibit 95); the Public Record Office, London (exhibit 105); the Society of Antiquaries of London (exhibit 48); the Ashmolean Museum, Oxford, Department of Western Art (exhibit 124); the Bodleian Library, Oxford, Department of Western Manuscripts (exhibit 32); Magdalen College, Oxford (exhibit 87); and Stanbrook Abbey, Worcester (exhibits 34 and 47). Further, Downside, the British Museum, Lambeth, the Public Record Office, the Society of Antiquaries, the Bodleian, and Magdalen College have allowed material in their keeping to be reproduced in the present book.

Especial thanks are due to Dom Philip Jebb, monk of Downside, Deputy Head Master of Downside School, and Archivist to the English Benedictine Congregation, and Dr David M. Rogers, Senior Assistant Librarian at the Bodleian Library, who accepted an invitation to arrange the section of the exhibition on the British Benedictines from 1600 to 1980 and have contributed the corresponding chapter, no. 7, to this book. Of the other chapters, nos 2, 5, and 6 are by Miss Rachel Stockdale and nos 1, 3, and 4 by D. H. Turner, both of the Department of Manuscripts, the Reference Division, the British Library.

D. H. Turner

'THIS LITTLE RULE FOR BEGINNERS'

THE excellence of the code for the religious life which he composed has earned for St Benedict the title of patriarch of western monasticism. Apart from what can be deduced from his rule virtually all there is to be known about his life is contained in the Dialogues of St Gregory the Great, pope from 590 to 604. St Gregory's Dialogues, so-called because they take the form of conversations between their author and his assistant, the deacon Peter, were written to solace the pontiff amidst the cares of administration by recalling the lives and miracles of Italians famous for virtue. The work has four books, of which the whole of the second is given to St Benedict, who also appears twice elsewhere. Exhibit 1 is a thirteenth-century copy of the Dialogues, from the library of Rochester Cathedral priory. It was either written there or acquired for the house, apparently whilst a monk whose name began with 'H' was precentor of Rochester, and consequently in charge of its books. In an initial at the beginning of the manuscript is a representation of St Gregory writing.

It is Benedict the wonder-worker whom Gregory describes. This is in accordance with the tenor of the Dialogues and it is difficult to construct a historical biography from what he says. Fabulous account though it may be, St Gregory's life of St Benedict became the model for saints' lives in the Middle Ages. Gregory cites four of Benedict's disciples as his authorities. This is in keeping with practice throughout the Dialogues, lest readers should doubt the miracles told.

Benedict was born c.480 at the town of Nursia, now Norcia, forty-one miles to the south-east of Perugia, of middle rather than upper class. He had a sister called Scholastica, who was to become a nun. Their world stood between ancient Greece and Rome and the Middle Ages. The Roman empire had collapsed in western Europe in 476, and survived in the eastern Mediterranean as the Byzantine empire.

Benedict was educated at Rome, but before completing his studies, decided to devote himself to the spiritual life. After a period with a rudimentary religious community at Enfide, some forty miles east of Rome, he became a hermit for several years in the nearby deserted locality of Subiaco. Inevitably, rumour spread of his holiness and a neighbouring monastery invited him to be their abbot. However, he alienated his subjects by his severity and withdrew back to Subiaco. The lesson of his first period as a religious superior may well account for much of the balance and moderation which were to characterize his rule. At Subiaco he could not remain hidden and for those who now sought him out as a guide he set up twelve monasteries, each with twelve men in them. He himself lived in a thirteenth, with some especially promising devotees. His reputation was such that noblemen of Rome sent their sons to Subiaco to be educated by him.

He was at Subiaco for some thirty years. Then, probably in 529, and prompted by differences with a local priest, who tried to murder Benedict, but who himself died tragically, Benedict removed with some of his followers to the place with which his memory is for ever linked, Monte Cassino, in Campania, on the main road from Rome to Naples [1]. The people there were still pagan and St Benedict converted them, building a monastery on the site of their temple, on the summit of the hill. There he died, traditionally on 21st March 543, in the oratory, supported on his feet and with his hands raised in prayer.

His remains were not destined to remain in peace. Monte Cassino was sacked by the Lombards c.580 and left deserted till refounded c.720. Although there has been much controversy about what happened, it appears that c.660 the relics of St Benedict and his sister St Scholastica, who had been buried in the same tomb, were removed to France and St Benedict's at least were taken to the monastery of Fleury-sur-Loire [2]. The standard account of the translation, and the most detailed and most fantastic, is by a ninth-century monk of Fleury, Adrevald (exhibit 4). He tells how the abbot of Fleury, encouraged by a vision, sent Aigulf, one of his monks, with some companions to find the body of Benedict. The expedition was enlarged by a party from the monastery of Le Mans on a similar quest and with similar supernatural backing. The two parties made common cause and course as far as Rome, where Aigulf gave the Le Mans monks the slip whilst they were occupied in sight-seeing, hurrying on south to Monte Cassino. Enabled by a vision to identify the grave of Benedict and Scholastica,

1. Monte Cassino. Photograph: Keystone Press Agency.

2. Fleury, St Benoit-sur-Loire. Photograph: French National Tourist Office.

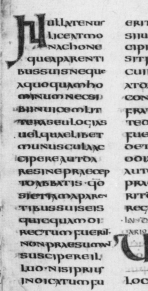

4. *The Hatton Rule of St Benedict, chapter liv and beginning of chapter lv.*

5. *Rule of St Benedict, beginning of prologue.*

he and his brethren had secured the relics before the Le Mans party arrived. The reunion between the two bands of relic-snatchers was scarcely happy, but Aigulf promised to be generous when they were all back at Fleury. There the Le Mans monks were finally allowed St Scholastica's bones. St Benedict's were enshrined at Fleury and 11th July is usually kept as the feast of this translation. There is also a feast of St Benedict on 4th December. Adrevald explains the July observance as the date on which the relics arrived at Fleury and the December one as that of the enshrinement there.

No contemporary likeness of St Benedict survives, nor was one probably made. In the exhibition are two later representations. That in the Benedictional of St Ethelwold (exhibit 33) will be discussed later. The other [3] is in a psalter (exhibit 3), which has twelfth-century additions. The original part was written at, and for, Christ Church Cathedral priory, Canterbury, by a monk of that house called Eadvius Basan, active as a scribe in the early eleventh century. It includes a liturgical calendar, which has the feast of St Alphege (19th May), archbishop of Canterbury, who was martyred by the Danes in 1012, as an original entry. The feast of his translation (8th June) in 1023, is a twelfth-century addition. Some fine illumination adorns the psalter, possibly the work of Eadvius. The minature of Benedict shows the saint himself and a monk embracing his feet, in full colour. To the right of them is a group of nine monks, done in tinted outline, the foremost of whom holds a copy of St Benedict's rule. The prostrate monk clasps a psalter, representing exhibit 3. He is meant for the man who 'made' this, either Eadvius Basan, or someone who commissioned him. The use of

◄ *3. Psalter, St Benedict and monks.*

line in the minature is lively and expressive, in the best tradition of Anglo-Saxon art of the century before the Norman Conquest. There is considerable characterization in the faces of the figures and the group of nine monks conveys a strong feeling of movement.

St Benedict's real portrait is in the rule which he wrote, c.526. It survives in three versions, the 'pure text', the 'interpolated text' and the 'received' or 'mixed' text. The 'pure text', of which only one copy is extant, in the famous library of the former monastery of St Gallen, in Switzerland, was probably unknown in England in the Middle Ages. The 'interpolated text' probably originated at Rome c.600 and was the recension common in the seventh and eighth centuries. Its oldest witness, indeed the oldest witness of the rule, was written in England, probably at Canterbury, at the beginning of the eighth century [4]. It is now amongst the treasures of the Bodleian Library at Oxford and is the only surviving manuscript of English origin of the 'interpolated text'. The 'received' text is a mixture of the 'pure text' and the 'interpolated text', due to the monastic reforms of the Emperor Louis the Pious and St Benedict of Aniane. From the mid-ninth century to the end of the nineteenth it was the standard recension. The oldest manuscript of it executed in England is in the British Library and is in the original part of the volume shown as exhibit 2 [5]. This material was written and illuminated c.1000, apparently at St Augustine's Abbey, Canterbury. It is bound up with items copied out in the thirteenth and fourteenth centuries. A fourteenth-century list of contents at the beginning of the volume shows that these were then as now. There is also an inscription of ownership by St Augustine's and the press-mark in the library there, 'Di. XIIII. Gra. I'. 'Di.' stands for 'distinctio', the Latin for book-case, and 'Gra.' for 'gradus', the Latin for book-shelf. Throughout the rule and the contemporary matter in exhibit 2 are decorated initials in black touched with red, employing mostly motifs of interlace, foliage, and birdlike or beastlike heads. Such initials are to be found in manuscripts of the period from all over southern England. The present ones are particularly good examples. The zoomorphic features stem from southern and midland English art of the eighth and ninth centuries, their leafwork from Carolingian art.

It is important to remember that St Benedict's rule was not written by a priest, but by a layman dedicated to the search for God, for a community composed mostly of laymen. Priests and clerics might join this community and members of it might be selected for ordination, but there was to be no distinction between them and the non-ordained in their status as monks. The assumption that a fully-fledged monk would also be a priest resulted from a gradual development, completed by about the middle of the twelfth century. Monastic engagement in pastoral work, particularly in the mission field, was decisive in this. Its corollary was the appearance of a class of lay-brothers, whose work was exclusively manual, whose share in the liturgical life was limited, and who had no say in the governance of the monastery.

No extramural work was to disturb St Benedict's ideal community. It was to be self-sufficient, under the paternal and absolute care of its abbot. The rule consists of a prologue and seventy-three chapters. The prologue, the last chapter, one on humility, two on the abbot, and one on 'if a brother be commanded to do impossibilities' are passages of the highest spirituality. The others range over a multitude of details, liturgical, administrative, and penal, but always maintaining an unmistakable flavour of spirituality and discretion. 'We have', says the prologue, 'to establish a school of the Lord's service in the institution of which we hope to order nothing that is harsh or rigorous'. The school is composed of cenobites, that is, religious who live in monasteries under a rule and an abbot. St Benedict contrasts this 'strongest type of monks' with the advanced life of anchorites and the degenerate life of monks who, 'tried by no rule nor by experience', follow their own desires, living 'in twos, or threes, or even singly', and the worse life of those monks 'who spend all their lives wandering . . . staying in different cells for three or four days at a time'. The idea of stability is fundamental to St Benedict's concept of the religious life. The society in which he lived knew no international or national organizations of religious.

For St Benedict a monk resided until death in the house where he was professed, and vowed so to do at his profession. He entered this house by one of two ways: by his own free choice as an adult, or by the choice of his parents as a child. The adult postulant, after perservering in spite of initial, explicitly ordered, rebuffs, served a year's novitiate. Persistence throughout this was rewarded by his profession, before all, in the oratory, when he took vows of stability, conversion of manners, and obedience. The profession of child postulants took place at once, when they were given by their parents to be brought up as monks, and their vows would be made on their behalf by their parents if necessary. The custom of child oblation accorded with the ideas about parental authority in St Benedict's time and was of venerable Christian antiquity. It survived amongst Benedictines till the mid-twelfth century, but there had been several moves by then to treat the original oblation as requiring ratification by its subject when he reached years of discretion.

The days of St Benedict's monks were divided between three activities. Four hours or so were occupied by liturgical prayer, about the same time by spiritual reading, and manual work took up six hours or so. The spiritual reading was not intellectual research and the manual work did not embrace all the agricultural labour needed to support the monastery. In this, non-monastic farm labourers helped. Also, those unwilling or unfitted for spiritual reading were to be assigned some other work. There were various officials in the monastery. There might be deans over sections in a large community. A cellarer, with assistants, looked after all the property. There was a guest-master, there might be a prior, there was a porter at the gate, and, above all, there was the abbot. 'He is believed to hold the place of Christ in the monastery'. He was elected for life by the community 'or even by a part, however small, with sounder counsel'. This seems to mean that in the absence of an absolute majority St Benedict preferred a simple relative one to a second scrutiny. The abbot appointed the other officials and was to be a living example of the rule, ever mindful that on the day of judgement he would have to give account for the souls committed to him. This solicitude for others should make him solicitous for himself. He should show forth all that is good or holy by his deeds, rather than his words, but not neglect to teach the intelligent by word of mouth. 'He must consider how difficult and arduous a task he has undertaken, of ruling souls and adapting himself to many dispositions'.

St Benedict firmly disavowed originality for his rule. It was 'a little rule for beginners' and he referred seekers after perfection to the teachings of the holy fathers

6. *St Augustine's Abbey, Canterbury: St Ethelbert's tower. Watercolour by W. A. Buckler.*

7. *Glastonbury Abbey: the exterior of the lady chapel. Watercolour.* ▶

and to the divinely inspired books of the Old and New Testaments. That he thought of himself as a legislator for the religious life, or was commissioned as such, is extremely unlikely. Religious communities in his day were essentially autonomous and independent, following a variety, or a mixture, of codes. This situation survives amongst Benedictines themselves to the extent that though all observe one rule, each of their houses is an independent, separate family under its own superior. There has never been a Benedictine order like there is one of Jesuits or Dominicans, centralized and uniform.

That there is a Benedictine order at all must be attributed in large part to St Gregory the Great, whose every work and writing is imbued with the spirit of St Benedict's rule. The future pope had converted his family mansion in Rome into a monastery of which he became a member and from which in 597 he sent its prior,

Augustine, with a band of monks to evangelize England. Augustine (d. between 604 and 609) became the first archbishop of Canterbury, but the success of his mission was limited and, as far as the religious life is concerned, resulted in only one foundation definitely, the monastery of Sts Peter and Paul, afterwards St Augustine's, at Canterbury [6]. The British Library has in its keeping a psalter which traditionally is one of a number of books sent by St Gregory to St Augustine. The tradition is found in the early fifteenth-century history of St Augustine's by Thomas of Elmham, monk of that house. In fact the psalter, known as the Vespasian Psalter, was written and illuminated in England in the first half of the eighth century, probably at Canterbury.

Neither at St Gregory's own monastery, St Andrew's, nor at St Augustine's is there evidence that the rule of St Benedict was the exclusive code. In England the early seventh century saw a strong wave of monasticism of the Celtic type spread over the north of the country from Iona. In the midlands at the same time several heterogeneous religious communities came into existence. The earliest recorded introduction of St Benedict's rule into Britain was by St Wilfrid (d. 709). Wilfrid, originally a monk of the Celtic foundation of Lindisfarne, had a chequered life. A convert to the ultra-montanism of his time, at the height of his career (669–677) he was bishop of York and a powerful figure in the politics of northern England, both lay and ecclesiastic. He had been given the monastery of Ripon c.661 and in 674 he founded one at Hexham. Monasteries of both men and women throughout the country placed themselves under his direction, thereby forming a congregation held together by a personal bond. St Wilfrid considered that the ordering of the observance of the rule of St Benedict by monks was one of his two chief achievements. He probably brought it to England when he returned from his first visit to the Continent and Rome in 653 to 658. Wilfrid's friend St Benedict Biscop (d. 689) certainly knew the rule and inspired his twin foundations of Wearmouth (674) and Jarrow (685) in Northumbria, with its spirit. He apparently learnt about it when he was monk of Lérins, on the island of that name off the south coast of France, from 665 to 667. However, on his deathbed he exhorted his disciples to keep the rule of life which he himself had given them, compiled from the customs of seventeen monasteries which he had visited.

Knowledge of St Benedict's rule was spreading in England in the later seventh and earlier eighth centuries and St Boniface, the apostle of Germany (d. 755), encountered it at Nursling, near Winchester, when he was a monk there in the first years of the eighth century. The first flowering of Benedictinism in Britain, and all regular religious life, was extinguished as a result of the Viking invasions of the ninth century.

The same century saw, on the continent of Europe, the elevation of the rule of St Benedict to universalism, by Louis the Pious, who ruled the Carolingian empire from 814 to 840, and his spiritual director St Benedict of Aniane (d. 821). On 10th July 817 they issued a set of edicts for monks, known as the Capitula of Aachen, based unequivocally on the rule of St Benedict. There are copies of the Capitula in the original part of exhibit 2 and in exhibit 7 in the exhibition. The system proposed by Louis and Benedict did not survive in the disintegration of the empire after Louis' death, but the example remained. A Benedictine order of monks was emerging, which received powerful impetus from the foundation of the monastery of Cluny in 910, the refoundation of Gorze c.933, and the foundation of Brogne c.920. All three houses had extensive influence and Cluny became the head of an actual international congregation. The emergent Benedictine order had important differences from St Benedict's Monte Cassino. Its monks were rarely, if ever, occupied in manual work. Their liturgical duties were increasing, intellectual pursuits were an accepted, even expected, part of their life and their houses were centres of civilization rather than retreats from it.

The British parallel to the Capitula of Aachen was the Regularis Concordia, issued at Winchester c.970. The occasion was a council of bishops, abbots, and abbesses, including St Dunstan, the archbishop of Canterbury, summoned by Edgar, king of England from 959 to 975 and recognized as overlord of Britain two years before his death. From the promulgation of the Concordia until c.1100, Benedictinism was the

8. Regularis Concordia, King Edgar with Sts Ethelwold and Dunstan.

9. *St Dunstan.*

norm for religious life in Britain. It remained a powerful force till the Reformation and subsequently it has not been without influence. The Concordia was the charter of a revival of religious life in England due to the initiative of three great men and saints, Dunstan, Ethelwold, and Oswald. In the early 940s Dunstan (b. *c.*909) was appointed abbot of the famed site of Glastonbury by Edgar's father Edmund, king of Wessex. What he found there was apparently a community of secular clerics and no monastic buildings. He built up a monastery in men and stones. The ruins of the abbey are shown in the exhibition in three anonymous, and so far unpublished, watercolours dating from the early nineteenth century (exhibits 11–13). The second and third [7] are of the lady chapel built *c.*1200 and the oldest building still standing at Glastonbury. All the early buildings were destroyed by fire in 1184. Exiled in 956, Dunstan was called to be bishop of Worcester in 957, London in 959, and primate in 961. He died in 988. Ethelwold had been one of his monks at Glastonbury. He became abbot of Abingdon *c.*954 and from 963 to his death in 984 he was bishop of Winchester. Oswald (d. 922) had been a monk at Fleury. In 961 he succeeded Dunstan as bishop of Worcester and in 972 became archbishop of York. The establishment of some thirty-four monasteries following the Benedictine rule is owed to the great three and it was Ethelwold who was the probable compiler of the Concordia.

This survives in only two manuscripts, both in the British Library. The later one is displayed as exhibit 7. It is part of a composite volume put together presumably by the antiquary Sir Robert Cotton. The portion of this containing the Regularis Concordia was executed probably at Christ Church Cathedral priory, Canterbury, in the second half of the eleventh century. There is an interlinear Anglo-Saxon translation to the Concordia and it is preceded by a tinted drawing [8] of King Edgar seated between presumably Sts Ethelwold and Dunstan. All three hold a scroll, presumably meant for the Concordia, and beneath them is a monk with another scroll. The drawing is very animated, as is obvious in the faces of the four figures, and even more in the posture of the monk, who could be said to be dancing. A more stylized rendering of St Dunstan is exhibit 5 [9], a miniature removed from exhibit 6, which is a late twelfth-century copy of the commentary on the rule of St Benedict by Smaragdus, abbot of St Mihiel (d. after 819). The Smaragdus was also done apparently at Christ Church, Canterbury and its St Dunstan and that in exhibit 7 make for a perfect comparison between the Anglo-Saxon painting which resulted from the monastic revival of the tenth century and Transitional painting in Britain. The Transitional style comes between Romanesque and Gothic, *c.*1180–1220, and is characterized by strong Byzantism and humanization of Romanesque abstractness. The basic difference between the miniature in exhibit 7 and exhibit 5 is that the first relies on a free use of lines and shades, the second on a contrived one.

Compared with other monastic customaries of the time the Regularis Concordia has some peculiarities. It includes an exhortation to daily communion and an incorporation of daily intercessions for the king and the queen as a prominent part of the liturgy. Nevertheless, the Concordia set up no English Benedictine congregation, although down to 1066 the Benedictine monasteries provided the leaders of the church of England and were the sole centres of learning in the country. After the Norman Conquest it was popular, and no doubt politic, to decry the old, Anglo-

Saxon, monasticism. There seems no basis of fact for this judgement. The Normaniza-tion of the English church, and its religious life, was a mixed blessing, which if it brought them immediately into more direct contact with the Continent, in the long run profoundly altered their character by feudalizing them. The eventual conse-quence of that was the Dissolution. The architect of the new church of England was Lanfranc, archbishop of Canterbury 1070 to 1089. Born at Pavia and trained as a lawyer, he became a monk at Bec, the most celebrated Benedictine abbey in Nor-mandy, c.1040. From 1066 to 1070 he was abbot of St Stephen's, Caen. His testament to the Benedictines in Britain is his Monastic Constitutions. These are addressed to the monastery which he ruled by right of being archbishop, Christ Church, Canterbury, although it seems that he hoped they would be a guide for others, as became the case. However, Lanfranc expressly states that circumstances prevent one church exactly imitating another and he clearly did not envisage imposition of his Constitutions throughout the country. It is from Cluny, rather than from Bec, that the Constitu-tions derive, although Lanfranc says that his compilation is from the customs of those monasteries which in his day have the greatest prestige. One source is conspicuously absent. That is the Regularis Concordia.

There is one copy of the Monastic Constitutions in the British Library, in exhibit 8. The volume of which they are part is composite, apparently put together by Sir Robert Cotton. The Constitutions once made up a volume with another manuscript in the Library, which includes a martyrology of Christ Church Cathedral priory, Canterbury, and a copy of the rule of St Benedict. This original volume was executed in the second quarter of the twelfth century, presumably at Christ Church. Two watercolours done in 1804 by J. Buckler have been selected for the exhibition to give visual reference to the Benedictine establishment which was for so long the chief church in England (exhibits 14 and 15) [10]. Canterbury Cathedral was certainly served by Benedictines before 1066 and it remained so till 1540. Cathedral monasteries were virtually an English peculiarity, going back to the introduction of monks at Winchester Cathedral by St Ethelwold and at Worcester Cathedral by St Oswald. Of the twenty-one cathedrals in existence in England and Wales at the Reformation, nine were staffed by Benedictine monks and one by Augustinian canons.

The generation after Lanfranc saw the new model of Cîteaux transform the religious life of the western church and in the thirteenth century the coming of the friars brought about an even more radical change. The Benedictines remained through the Middle Ages and the Renaissance as the senior type of religious, both male and female, but rather aristocratic and established, scarcely anymore in the forefront of the spiritual combat. In 1215 the Lateran Council united the Benedictines of each ecclesiastic province into a body, with a triennial meeting of their superiors and visitors for houses of both men and women. In 1336 Pope Benedict XII issued a set of decrees for organization of the Benedictine order, the most important of which for the black monks in England was the uniting into one congregation of those in the provinces of Canterbury and York. A copy of the decrees is in exhibit 9 and in exhibit 10 is an account of the first meeting of the provincial chapter of the English Benedictines at the Cluniac priory at Northampton in 1338. The constitutional apparatus set up by the Lateran Council and Benedict XII survived until the Dissolu-

10. Canterbury: the remains of Christ Church Cathedral priory. Watercolour by J. Buckler.

tion. The last recorded meeting of the English provincial chapter before the Dissolution was in 1532 at Westminster. Of the Benedictine polity in Britain after the Reformation Dom Philip Jebb and Dr David Rogers will speak.

'The letter killeth, but the spirit giveth life.' Legal documents are notoriously not mines of spiritual inspiration. Lanfranc's Constitutions, the Regularis Concordia, and like decretals, in Britain and elsewhere, were mostly expansions and explications of St Benedict's rule for different and more complicated times and circumstances. Even some religious rules are little more than organizational codes. St Benedict's stands out as a compendium of things spiritual and temporal, in general and in detail. That the observance of it leads to the heights can be deduced from St Gregory. He tells how one night at prayer St Benedict saw a light brighter than that of the day and in it the whole world as it were gathered within the compass of one ray of the sun. The symbolism and the nature of the vision are those of the enlightenment of all who have explored consciousness to the utmost. At all times and in all places there have been those who seek to 'go they know not where by a road they know not of'. The roads are many, but the end the same. Understandably those who have travelled the roads have wished to leave behind a guide-book for others. One of the finest guide-books is St Benedict's. Some monks and nuns have used it well, some badly, some indifferently. Benedictines have done many works. They have built buildings, they have painted pictures, they have composed music, they have written books — both ones of their own composition and ones passing on the wisdom of others — but the criterion of a Benedictine remains one and the same. It is that for which St Benedict directs the novice-master to watch in his novices, 'whether he really seeks God'.

Rachel Stockdale

'A SCHOOL OF THE LORD'S SERVICE'

'WE have to establish a school of the Lord's service, in the institution of which we hope to order nothing that is harsh or rigorous.' St Benedict's words in his prologue to the rule indicate his belief that monastic life should be a discipline, a continuing education with the implicit aim of achieving self-respect, a responsible attitude towards others, and a proper relationship with God. Serving the Lord lends itself to different levels of interpretation: for some it may be the humble completion of daily tasks, for others, the fulfillment of a particular role as abbot or official of the community, for a few, the representation of monastic interests in the wider ecclesiastical or secular world. This chapter is concerned with aspects of the interrelated ideas of education and service, as reflected in the lives of the ordinary monk and his abbot, and in the organization of the community as a whole.

There were two points of entry to the monastic training course: at the age of about seven, the candidate might be presented by his parents as an oblate (see chapter 1), or he might wait until adulthood at about eighteen years to express his own desire to join the community. Child oblation was widespread and accepted among Benedictines until the twelfth century, although the Cistercians and the newer orders rejected it. Lanfranc weakened its significance by insisting that only a preliminary promise was involved, which had to be confirmed by the customary profession when the child came of age.

The essential sanction provided by the rule was that admission to the monastic community should not be too easy. The postulant had to make his request four or five times before he was allowed to stay in the guest house for a few days as an observer. After that, he could mix with the other novices, but not with the fully professed brethren. A senior monk or 'novice-master' was deputed to show him the hardships and trials ('dura et aspera') of his chosen way of life, and to test his motives to see if he were genuinely seeking God. At intervals of two months, six months and four months, the rule was read aloud to him, and he was given the formal choice between agreeing to observe it or leaving the community. If he proved steadfast throughout this period, he was considered eligible for full admission. Later practice, influenced by Lanfranc's reforms, modified the fixed year's noviciate and allowed the abbot and his advisers to determine when a postulant's conversion seemed complete.

Within the general framework of the rule, each house could institute its own methods of training. Exhibit 16 gives a detailed picture of the novice's life at St Augustine's Abbey, Canterbury about 1330. Three days before admission, the new entrants were invited to dine with the abbot and were introduced to their novice-master who was responsible for their material needs. During the preliminary days, he prepared them for confession and instructed them in the rudiments of liturgical ceremonial. The day of admission began with attendance at mass, until the elevation of the host when the novices were required to withdraw. After the service, they were taken to the chapter, and they prostrated themselves while the abbot made formal enquiry as to what they wanted. The prior answered on behalf of them all, 'We desire the grace of God.' The abbot then warned of the hardships and trials of monastic life and posed three conventional questions: were they free-born, were they in good health, and were they prepared to take the rough with the smooth, to sustain obedience and to endure abuse for the love of Christ and their own salvation? If the proper response was given, 'Yes, by the grace of God', the abbot proceeded with further questions: had they ever been professed in any other order, had they ever entered any marriage contract, had they any debts, and had they ever been guilty of any major breach of law? A negative answer was expected, 'No, by the grace of God'. With this proof of their sincerity and suitability the abbot granted their request for admission and commended them to God. As a symbol of their new status, the novices were shaved and dressed in a distinctive habit and they returned to their master for further instruction. Spiritual and social behaviour were regulated in detail during the noviciate, and attitudes were instilled which were to remain with the monk throughout his life. The Instruction of Novices in exhibit 16 explains such matters as table manners ('no-one may drink until a signal is given'), conduct in the cloister, order of precedence, hygiene ('the hair must be combed before prime except on Good Friday'), respect for the abbot, use of service books and changing of clothes ('clothes must only be changed on the appointed day, except in cases of urgent necessity'). The novice-master was to supervise his charges at all times and to see that the rules were obeyed.

The end of the first stage of training and entry upon a stricter discipline was marked by the solemn profession, in which the novice made his commitment to the monastic life, symbolically cast off his old ways and adopted the new with the assumption of the full habit, and received a blessing from his superior. A number of manuscripts bears witness to changes in the detail of the ceremony over a long period, but its essentials remained the same. The pre-Conquest version is found in exhibit 17, a pontifical or bishop's service-book. A statement that the vow was made 'in the presence of the lord archbishop' connects the volume indubitably with Christ Church, Canterbury, the only house in England in the mid-eleventh century which was ruled by an archbishop. The instructions begin on the page previous to that reproduced in [11]. The novice had first to be examined in his knowledge of the rule by his master.

Having passed this test, he was allowed to prostrate himself before the abbot and brethren in chapter with a formal request to join the community. If it were granted, he kissed the abbot's feet and bowed in gratitude to the other monks. The Latin words of the profession had to be copied out in advance of the ceremony, by the candidate himself if he were literate, or by someone else on his behalf. On the appointed day, mass was celebrated, but before the gospel reading, the candidate approached the altar and made his profession aloud: 'I, brother X, dedicated to God, promise my stability, the conversion of my life, and obedience according to the rule of St Benedict the abbot, before God and his saints in the presence of the lord archbishop.' The wording of the vow, except for the final phrase, was almost identical with that prescribed by St Benedict. In the eighth and early ninth centuries, it was common practice to vow only stability and obedience, but the earlier form, including 'conuersio morum' (or sometimes 'conuersatio morum') was restored during the ninth century. Of the three traditional vows of a religious, only obedience was normally promised in the Benedictine profession, poverty and chastity being implicit in the acceptance of the whole rule. Stability was a fundamental concept in St Benedict's ideal: the monk should not leave his own monastery, nor desire to do so, unless sent out on specific business by a superior. 'Conversion of life' meant the acceptance of the rule and the intention to live by it, symbolized in the act of taking the habit, and obedience involved loyalty to the abbot and community as well as the ultimate obedience to God.

With his own hand, the candidate placed the parchment bearing his written profession upon the altar. Bowing to all sides, he sang a verse from Psalm cxviii, 'Suscipe me domine secundum eloquium tuum, et uiuam; et non confundas me ab expectatione mea.' The congregation replied with the same verse, usually repeated three times. In English versions of the ceremony, the candidate lay prostrate while the abbot intoned the 'Kyrie eleison' and the congregation supplied the appropriate responses. The blessing of the cowl occupied the second part of the service. The prayers associated with it were open to choice and a set form was only established towards the end of the Middle Ages. In the present manuscript, four prayers asking for God's help for the new monk precede the blessing, and others on a similar theme follow it, with antiphons and responses, some of them optional. The monk put on the full habit as a symbol of the 'new man', and the abbot personally placed the cowl over his head. In the earliest versions, the ceremony ended with the long prayer, 'Omnipotens et misericors deus', but by the eleventh century, a more or less elaborate benediction formed the usual conclusion. However, the order of service was far from invariable.

The newly professed monk needed guidance both in spiritual matters and in the rules of his house. Exhibits 18, 19 and 20 are examples of the books from which he might draw such guidance. Spiritual strength was to be derived from private prayer, recommended by St Benedict but not regulated in detail, presumably to safeguard its spontaneity. The mind attuned to the repetition of the medieval liturgy, however, needed some focus of concentration, even for informal prayer, a need which could be met by the use of small personal prayer-books such as exhibits 18 and 19. Originally a single volume, these books were prepared for Aelfwine, dean and later abbot of the New Minster, Winchester, by a fellow monk, Aelsine, as explained in a cryptographic distich and statement on folio 13b of the second volume: 'Frater humillimus

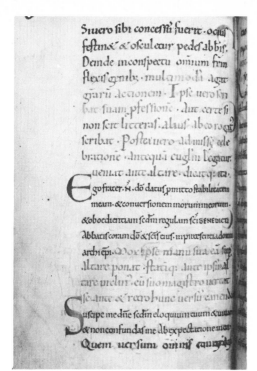

11. Pontifical, ceremony of monastic profession.   *12. The Prayer-book of Aelfwine, St Peter.*

et monachus Aelsinus me scripsit' *etc.* The calendar notes the dates of death of members of Aelfwine's family, his father, mother, three sisters and brother, and it incidentally reveals his own promotion to abbot. The prayer-book is a curious mixture of devotions of various kinds, supplemented with computistical, astrological and liturgical memoranda. Although less sumptuous than the books of the communal offices, it is pleasingly written with coloured initials and rubrics and three full-page drawings, which represent a late development of the Rheims style of Carolingian art. The drawing of St Peter, patron of the New Minster, is firm in its line and is shaded tastefully in green, blue, yellow and red [12]. The saint is seated between two columns, holding his keys in his right hand and a book in his left, while a suppliant monk is at his feet. The Crucifixion scene is unusual in its portrayal of the sun and moon above the arms of the cross as three-quarter length classical figures. Mary and John stand below against a background of feathery plants, and the hand of God issues in benediction from the clouds. Aelfwine is mentioned again in the inscription. The shading is predominantly green, with lines of red, brown and blue.

Despite the centralizing influence of someone like Lanfranc, individual abbots were able to mitigate the severity of the rule by instituting their own 'house-rules' in matters of ceremony, discipline and diet. These rules were committed to writing in books known as customaries and became the accepted code of practice for the house. An example is found in the Liber Albus of Bury St Edmunds (exhibit 20), under the heading 'Traditiones patrum' (the practice of the elders), the very terminology used by St Benedict when he recommended that established custom be respected. The content of the Bury customary ranges from the administration of manors to the entertainment of guests (the status of a visitor and scale of hospitality accorded to him to be determined by the number of horses in his retinue), liturgical observances, the infirmary, punishments, the duties of various officers, precedence, food and drink, and the ceremonies connected with death. The comments on food refute the notion that the monastic diet was always frugal. From Easter until 13th September when herrings were served at the main midday meal, three fish were to be provided for each monk. From 14th September until the day before the Monday of Quadragesima, each individual was to have four, and from then until the Vigil of Easter, five. At the lighter evening meal, they were restricted to two herrings each throughout the year. Further directions were given as to whether the fish should be fresh or salted and how it should be cooked, followed by instructions regarding vegetables and bread, with punishment prescribed for any baker who dared to deliver short measure.

The personal qualities and method of election of an abbot or prior according to the rule have been discussed in chapter 1. A special blessing for the abbot-elect was suggested both by St Benedict and by St Gregory, and this blessing developed into a complete rite of consecration similar to that bestowed on a new bishop. The Anderson Pontifical, exhibit 46 [13], describes the ceremony as performed probably at Winchester about the year 1000. In the manuscript, feminine forms of the key words have been written between the lines to adapt the text for the consecration of an abbess. The officiating bishop, normally the diocesan, began by asking for God's gracious approval of the nominee in the words of the prayer, 'Concede quaesumus omnipotens deus'. Sometimes, although not in the present version, he presented a copy of the Benedictine rule to the new abbot, with an injunction to observe its precepts. Divine approval was to be manifested in help and protection, as requested in the next two prayers, 'Deus qui sub tuae maiestatis arbitrio' and 'Super hunc famulum tuum'. Then appropriate symbols of office were presented and their significance explained: first the pastoral staff with the words, 'Accipe baculum pastoralis officii et monastici regiminis', and secondly the ring with the words, 'Accipe anulum discretionis et honoris integre fidei signaculum'. The texts referring to the staff and ring have been added in the margins of the Anderson Pontifical. Prayers for God's blessing and bestowal on the abbot of the qualities necessary for his new duties, and a formal benediction completed the consecration. In this early Anglo-Saxon rite, there is no evidence of the elaborate ceremonial which accompanied later consecrations, such as the abbot's removing his shoes on entering the church, nor is there any vow of obedience to the bishop.

To perform his liturgical and administrative duties, the abbot required certain books which might be made within the monastery to his own specifications. The service-book appropriate to his particular functions was the ritual, which contained the priestly offices. Exhibit 47 is a modern Rituale Abbatum, printed in 1963 by the Benedictine nuns of Stanbrook Abbey, Worcestershire. It is an outstanding example of fine printing, on handmade paper with a binding of parchment and red leather.

13. The Anderson Pontifical, the blessing of an abbot. ▶

militanſ. tuæ maieſtatiſ mereatur ubiq̆. clypeo
pacifico   ptegı. Dextera tuæ diuinitatıſ eum dıg
neriſ locupletare. utopem frugale fratrıb; inferre.
&omnıb; undıq̆. aduenientıb; pıe poſſıt pfutura
exhıbere. Tu illı eſto honor. tu gaudıum indomo.
inıtınere ſocıuſ. inmerore ſolacıum. inambıgui
tate conſılıum. inegritudıne medıcına· inlaboꝛı
buſ adıutor: inaduerſıſ defenſoꝛ. intrıbulatıone
patıentıa ; Ponat inte puidentıam mentıſ. ꝑte
dıſcat cum conſılıo commıſſı ſıbı gregıſ gubernacula
ſapıent moderari. utſemp felıx. ſemperq̆. exul
tanſ. detuæ bonıtatıſ dıtatıſ beneficııſ mereat
gaudere. & plıxıtate preſenaſ uıtæ ꝑtemporalıa
bona benıgne ſuſcıpe. ac ſupernıſ cıuıb; angeloruq̆.
choꝛıſ peræterna commercıa copularıp ALIA.
unctorum, inſtıtutoꝛ dſ. quıp moyſen famulu tuu
adgubernandaſ æcleſ ꝑpoſıtoſ inſtıtuıſtı. tıbı
ſupplıceſ fundımuſ pceſ teq̆. deuotıſ mentıb; exo
ramuſ uthıc famuluſ tuıuſ, quem conıbentıa &electıo
famuloꝛ tuoꝛ abbatem hodıe ouıum tuaru .ẽẽ.
inſtıtuıt. ſıc regat ſubdıtoſ. commendatoſ. utcu
illıſ omnıb; regna celoꝛ adıpıſcatur. quatınuſq̆.

Sup hunc famulũ tuũ dñe qſ.
HIC DETUR BACULUS. ETDICAT
EPS ABBATI.

Accıpe baculũ paſtoralıſ
officıı & monaſtıcı regımınıſ
& ſıſ ıncorrıgendıſ uıtııſ ſeuı
ınıra ıudıcıum ſıne ıra tem
cum ıratuſ fuerıſ. mıſerıcoꝛ
remınıſcenſ; Accıpe ınquı
baculũ. ſacrı moderamınıſ
ſıgnũ. ut ınbecılleſ conſol
deſ. tıtubanteſ conſırmeſ.
prauoſ corrıgaſ. rectoſ dırıga
ın uıa ſalutıſ eterne. preſta
dño nro ıhu xpo q̃ cũ patre &
ſpu ſco uıuıt & regnat dſ.

14. *The Lindesey Psalter, the Crucifixion.*

Three orders of service are included: those for receiving a postulant to the monastic habit, for receiving a novice to initial profession and for receiving a junior to solemn profession. The main text is printed in black, with red initials at the beginning of each paragraph and rubrics or instructions in red. The accentuation of the words is marked to facilitate reading aloud, the incipits of musical verses are quoted, and plural forms are included in brackets where applicable.

Similarly representative of the finest craftsmanship of its period is the Lindesey Psalter (exhibit 48). An inscription on the fly-leaf tells that it was once the property of Robert of Lindesey, abbot of Peterborough from 1214 to 1222, whose name is linked with strict adherence to the Benedictine rule and profitable management of the monastic farm. It is recorded that he had a personal collection of seven books, including a glossed psalter (probably to be identified with a manuscript now at St John's College, Cambridge) and an unglossed psalter (the present exhibit). Peterborough, under a succession of enlightened abbots, produced a number of illuminated psalters in the thirteenth century, of which this is the earliest extant. Its date can be fixed between 1220, the translation of St Thomas Becket, the entry of which feast is in the calendar, and 1222, the year when Lindesey himself died. Accurate dating is significant in consideration of the illustrations, which represent both old and new styles. Six tinted outline drawings on folios 33-34, portraying scenes from the life of Christ, reflect the older tradition of rigid drapery and set facial expressions. The historiated initials and two full-page miniatures, however, are masterpieces of thirteenth-century skill, with their symmetrical composition, expressively posed figures and dramatic use of space, heightened by strong colours and intricately tooled gold backgrounds. The foliated cross in the Crucifixion scene [14] is unusual and impressive, its arms extending into and blending with the deep blue inner border of the frame.

The ritual and psalter are typical abbot's books, designed for an obvious purpose. The Sherborne Chartulary (exhibit 49) is a unique book which presents problems at a first glance. Its title is misapplied, since only the first half of the volume is a chartulary or collection of charters. They relate to Sherborne and its cell at Horton in Dorset, and so indicate the provenance of the compilation. The second half is a purely liturgical work, a set of gospels and collects whose character makes it clear that they were intended for the use of an abbot, presumably Peter of Sherborne who ruled the house during the early 1140s when the book would seem to have been made. An explanation for this curious juxtaposition of the secular and liturgical lies in the sanctity attributed to an altar book, and in a contemporary ecclesiastical controversy. The monastery of Sherborne was in dispute with Jocelin, bishop of Salisbury over jurisdiction within the see, and in 1145 the pope settled the matter with a ruling in favour of Sherborne which was confirmed by a papal bull. Delighted at their success, the monks were anxious that all the evidence relating to the quarrel and its resolution, both ancient and contemporary, should be preserved for posterity, in case at some future time the rights of Sherborne should again be questioned. In the eleventh and twelfth centuries, important documents of legal significance were sometimes copied out on blank pages of gospel books, for such books were kept on the high altar of the church and were unlikely to be destroyed or tampered with deliberately. The Sherborne Chartulary is perhaps the only surviving evidence of an attempt to preserve a complete record in this way and to make it an integral part of the volume. Ignorance of this purpose caused the order of the leaves to become confused during rebinding, and it was not until the manuscript came to the British Museum that the original composition was recognized and the proper order restored. The illumination and initials are in a style typical of a twelfth-century liturgical manuscript, but the iconography is unusual. St John, for example [15], is portrayed as a standing figure, a pose normally reserved for prophets. In his attitude, as well as in his dark, almost Byzantine features and the folds of his clothing, he has been compared with the figure of Moses in the Bury Bible. He is identified by a gold nimbus and a book from which issue the opening words of his gospel.

An abbot or prior, once appointed, usually served in this capacity for life, as depositions and voluntary resignations were very rare. The death of the head of a house occasioned mourning and special prayers, not only in his own community, but among neighbours from a wide area. To announce the event, an obituary roll might be drawn up by the precentor and taken from house to house by a brief-bearer, a layman appointed under special licence. Exhibit 51, the second oldest surviving English obituary roll, commemorates Lucy, the foundress and first prioress of the Benedictine nunnery of Hedingham in Essex, who died c.1230. The roll opens with three tinted drawings: The Virgin and Child and Crucifixion, two angels bearing Lucy's soul to heaven, and her body in a coffin being censed and asperged [16]. A circular letter in the names of the new prioress Agnes and the rest of the community announces the death, emphasizing the grief of the nuns and praising Lucy's virtues, her chastity, sanctity and good example, with a word play on her name ('lucis scientia'), and the conventional request for prayers. The letter is written in a good bookhand. Each of the monasteries among which the roll was circulated added its own *titulus,* usually in cursive script and in conventional form: the name of the house and its patron saint, the order, diocese and sometimes the county, a prayer that the soul of the deceased might rest in peace, and a stereotyped request for reciprocal prayers, 'Vestri nostra damus, pro nostris uestra rogamus.' One hundred and twenty-two establishments are represented on this roll, ranging through central and southern England from Norfolk to Dorset and including one newly-founded Franciscan house at Cambridge. The continuation of the practice in post-Reformation mortuary bills can be seen in Chapter 7 and exhibit 122.

A meritorious abbot might be commemorated in a stone effigy, like the five which can still be seen at Peterborough, or from the early thirteenth century, in a sepulchral brass. Ironically, only a small proportion of these supposedly permanent memorials to ecclesiastics survived the Reformation. One of the largest and finest brasses extant in England is that of Thomas de la Mare in St Albans Abbey. Its size and style, the main figure engraved on a solid brass plate whose background is incised with trefoils and dragons, the surrounding canopy crowded with smaller figures of prophets, saints and angels, suggest that it was manufactured in north Germany or Flanders, probably during the lifetime of its subject. Exhibit 36 [17] is a nineteenth-century rubbing. De la Mare, who died in 1396, was a mitred abbot, entitled to use pontifical vestments and insignia. His full ceremonial dress, accurately represented on the brass, consisted

15. The Sherborne Chartulary, St John the Evangelist.

16. Obituary roll of Lucy, foundress and first prioress of Castle Hedingham, Lucy's soul being carried to heaven and her body in its coffin.

of the sacerdotal garments, the amice, alb, stole and maniple, over which were worn the pontifical tunicle and dalmatic. A rich chasuble with two humeral orphreys hung loosely on top. Silk gloves and sandals were additional symbols of pontifical privilege. The mitre and crozier, together with the ring which cannot be seen on the brass, completed the insignia.

Vestments are the subject of the exhibited folios of the memorandum-book of Henry of Eastry, prior of Christ Church, Canterbury (exhibit 61). Folio 115b has an inventory of stoles and maniples, followed by a list of the vestments in the charge of the four subsacrists. On folio 116 [18] is a rubric, 'Noua uestimenta oblata tempore H. prioris', that is, a list of vestments donated during Henry's own period of rule as prior, 1285–1331. They include the regalia of Archbishop Peckham, a chasuble, tunicle and dalmatic of red cloth decorated in gold, several items formerly owned by Robert of Winchelsey, and garments that had once belonged to King Philip of France, embroidered with the royal fleur-de-lys. Vestments commissioned for the priory at the time of Henry constitute the next section. The first three sets (at the bottom of [18]) are designated 'Vestimentum eiusdem H.' which suggests that they were worn and donated by the prior himself.

The richness of the vestments reflects the wealth of Christ Church in the early

17. Rubbing of the sepulchral brass of Thomas de la Mare, abbot of St Albans.

18. Memorandum-book of Henry of Eastry, prior of Christ Church, Canterbury, lists of vestments.

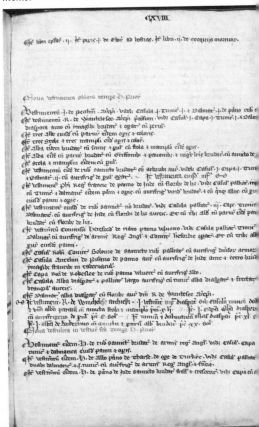

fourteenth century, a wealth due almost entirely to Henry's own efforts. Whilst the economy of the Benedictine order is too vast a subject to be treated within a limited compass, it is perhaps not unjust to let Henry's work stand as a representative example, the financial achievement of one outstanding prior who regarded his service to God in practical terms. On the day of his election, according to one of his notes, the house had debts of £5,000, or more than twice the yearly income. Henry saw the solution to the problem and set about implementing it with characteristic energy. He reduced waste and unnecessary expenditure. He reorganized and took personal control of the administration of Christ Church and its estates. He developed the existing treasury of the monastery and overhauled the auditing system. He pursued a 'scientific' farming policy, suiting the crop to each type of land and selling the produce with an eye to the advantages of the market. His methods were recorded in the varied content of the memorandum-book: detailed taxation records, notes on administrative procedure, inventories, a catalogue of books in the library, lists of animals and crops, household requisites, accounts, copies of charters and statutes affecting Christ Church and its possessions, notes of new building projects undertaken by himself and lands which he acquired. The result of his efforts could be seen in the golden age of prosperity enjoyed by Christ Church, which raised it even above the great Cistercian houses whose names were synonymous with sound economy.

Informal records like Henry of Eastry's memorandum-book are comparatively rare. Most of the evidence of Benedictine business activity in the Middle Ages survives in the formal documents, above all in charters and chartularies. Item 55 [19] is a royal grant of land at Madingley in Cambridgeshire, made in 975 by King Edgar to Ethelwold, bishop of Winchester. The essential element in the transaction was the livery of seisin, or physical act of handing over a piece of turf from the property. The charter was merely a record of the act drawn up by a royal clerk and naming those present as witnesses, Dunstan, archbishop of Canterbury, Oswald, archbishop of York and Ethelwold among others. The witnesses did not sign their own names or even make their own marks on the document. Conveyance of land between monastic houses is exemplified by exhibit 60 [20], a charter by which Peter, prior of the Benedictine abbey of Bath granted some of its property to the Cistercians of Margam in Glamorganshire for an annual rent of five shillings. The document was made as a three-part indenture, cut with a wavy line on the left-hand side, and through the word 'cirographum' across the top. It bears two seals in red wax, their tags slotted together in a curious fashion. The first seal of the chapter of Bath, depicting part of the building with an inscription in Saxon letters, was probably made from an early-tenth-century matrix which had been in use since the refounding of the abbey. The pointed oval seal of Robert of Lewes, bishop of Bath and Wells, shows a typical pontifical standing figure, full-length, with pastoral staff and hand raised in benediction. Exhibit 64, a charter of about a century later, records a transaction between Simon of Luton, abbot of Bury St Edmunds, and Walter of Luton, in which a piece of land in Suffolk changed hands for an annual rent of twenty-two pence. This abbot used his personal seal which carried on the obverse a standing figure in an architectural setting, intended to represent the abbey, and on the reverse, a smaller oval counterseal [21] showing the decapitation of St Edmund and the wolf guarding his head, with above, a half-length portrait of the Virgin and Child.

Religious houses needed their own seals to authenticate the documents which they issued. A design incorporating architectural features of the building, not always accurate, and perhaps a representation of its patron saint was a typical choice (exhibits 58 and 59 [22]). The abbot was officially keeper of the seal until 1307, when a law compelling all monasteries to acquire a conventual seal also imposed certain safeguards on its custody. The matrix had to be kept locked away, with three or four senior monks acting as key-holders, and in theory, all leases and grants, even those of

P Innomine dī summi eelsissimi iħu xp̄i tgregius azomista frumoematus ē Inscriptupaī ōiuuinī scē p̄
dicenf omnia nuda ceapreica ... etiam oculf ōi p̄pima usque concieniū uniuf cuiusq̄; actuf p̄pof
quandam junuf papciculum ... manuī Inuillam que abeiuſdem paẓur Incolif madanlitg nuncupa
qui ab unuſce paẓur gooſ boi nebili aſelpolo apellacaū onomace p̄o obſequio ruf deuoaſſimo p̄
epiſcopi cum omnibuſ ueenſibuſ p̄uaceī uidelicee paſcuuf ſiluſ uoa compoſ habeae te poſe uiuae
nomiſ Inmunem deielinquae Sie auceṃ p̄pdie tum juſ omni cempeue ſequiruruſ luẓo liberum eul
apeiſue pſaupaaone Siquiſ igceui hane n̄am donaaonem Inaliud quam conſtiuimuſ eian
eepuṃiſ bapeachiu Incendiſ luẓubiuſ luẓeaṃ cumuda xp̄i p̄edieoie euſquṛ compliabuſ puuma
ẓuua quod conepa n̄um deliquie deeiueaum hiſ meaſ p̄pfeacum juſ hine Inde ẓipaaṃ ·:·

Diſſundon þa land ẓemeiuo eo madan leaẓe eipeſe on picena leaẓe Incapadel oeṛapadele inpiuman poþ oþppuman poþda ono
bace oþþan bace onfone heẓe oþþon heẓe on pilbunẓe peẓe oþ þaṃ peẓe Incapeſihean pyll oþþannpylle Inþadie oþ þeiuedie In
poþda onfone hpaodihean moṛ oþþon moṛe In þa heþihean leẓe oþþeiue leẓe In þa hyiſce onſaẓiueacan ae oþ þeiue ae hṛiſ ſie oþ

Annoeomince Incaiunaaoniſ dcccc lxxiiii ſcupea eſe hee capea hiſ eeſtibuſ conſmoenabuſ quoru

✝ Ego EADGAR rex p̄pfacum donaaonem conſenſi ·
✝ Ego dunſean dopouernenſiſ æcclesie apcheī ep̄ſ eſignaui ·
✝ Ego oſpold eboraeenſiſ æcclesie apcheī ep̄ſ con ppimaui ·

✝ Ego aþelpolo ·	ep̄ſ	conceſſi ·	✝ Ego alfþryþ	reẓina	✝ Ego
✝ Ego alppold ·	ep̄ſ	eppimaui ·	✝ Ego æſcpiẓ ·	abbod ·	✝ Ego
✝ Ego ælfſean ·	ep̄ſ	eoṛpoboṛaui ·	✝ Ego ælfpic ·	abbod ·	✝ Ego
✝ Ego pynſiẓe ·	ep̄ſ	conſolidaui ·	✝ Ego oſẓaṛ ·	abbod ·	✝ Ego l
✝ Ego aþulf ·	ep̄ſ	adquieui ·	✝ Ego aþelẓaṛ	abbod ·	✝ Ego
✝ Ego ſyðeman ·	ep̄ſ	adppimaui ·	✝ Ego ſiẓaṛ ·	abbod ·	✝ Ego

the abbot's own lands, had to be approved by the community as a whole. In addition, the abbot might have a personal seal which could be used alone or as a counterseal on the back of the conventual seal. Like that of a bishop it was usually of a pointed oval shape and displayed a standing figure. In larger monasteries, some other officers might find it necessary to have seals.

The personal seal of Abbot de la Mare is attached to exhibit 62. It is a good impression in red on a mass of uncoloured wax, depicting the abbot against the architectural background of his abbey, wearing his mitre and vestments and holding a book and crozier (the brass-rubbing, exhibit 36, may be compared). Representations of the martyrdoms of St Thomas Becket, St Alban and possibly St Amphibalus are incorporated

20. *Grant by the prior and community of Bath Cathedral priory to the abbey of Margam.*

21. *Seal of Simon ▶ of Luton, abbot of Bury St Edmunds, reverse.*

19. *Grant by King Edgar to St Ethelwold.*

22. *Second seal of Norwich Cathedral priory, obverse.*

Ego	Aðelſtan	dux.		Ego	henulf	diac.
Ego	Eadpulf	dux.		Ego	Alfſtan	diac.
Ego	Oidulf	dux.		Ego	Aðeculf	diac.
Ego	Elfſtan	dux.		Ego	Wilfred	min.
Ego	Cuðped	dux.		Ego	Beophtnoð	min.
Ego	Tunbeoʒd	abb.		Ego	Aðelnoð	min.
Ego	Alfred	pb.		Ego	Dudiʒ	min.
Ego	huntʒiʒ	pb.		Ego	hepernoð	min.
Ego	Cyneſtan	pb.		Ego	Aðelpeoð	min.
Ego	Biopnlaf	pb.		Ego	Alphepe	min.
				Ego	Signed	min.

ÐES londeſ ʒe meno æt EASTVNE. hið of yccenan in eanna bæce æft ſpa 7
lanʒ bæceſ. uto on ðæt ʒeat æft be han and heafdan oð þone midleſtan beopʒ. æft
ſpa on cedeſpyrðe eaſte peapde æft uto on ſa poda on hepin ʒeleah eaſte peapdue. æft
uto on þa ſuþ on ſmalan dune eaſtepeapde. æft uto on þa ſuþ ðæ pulfped het. adnifan
æft of dune on ða dene ſpa on ðone mylen ſteall æt ſpe of ðem mylen ſtealle and lanʒ yccenan
æft on eanna bæce.

Dur iſ ðretumeſ land boc 7 þana rehida ſpurulinʒ þe eʒbyrht cuninʒ ʒeſealde
into ealdan mynſtre on pinceaſtre wiþ hiſ ſaple aliʒedneſſa
ʒode to lufe 7 to puldre 7 hiſ eadʒian apoſtolæ ſce petre
7 ſce paule on ece yſſeſ.

ETERIS AC NOVI

TESTAMENTI PANDIT AVCTORITAS. AVOD QVIDA SALVATORIS ET DNI
nri ihu xpi diſpenſatio omneſ ſcoſ ſuoſ ad uitam eternam prordinatoſ ante mundi
conſtitutionem elegit. exquibʒ uniuerſali eccle quam ſanguine ſuo redemit duo luminaria
ppoſuit beatum ſcilicet aptorum principem petrum. eʒ coapłm eiuſ ſaulum. quibʒ ſpe
tialiter incelo eʒ in terra ligandi ſoluendiʒ poteſtatem conceſſit. ut fideleſ quoſeʒ pro bonorʒ
opum meritiſ meritia tabnacula recipiant. infideleſ autem eʒ ueritatiſ aduerſarioſ ab in
greſſu regni celeſtiſ ſolo ſermone repellant. Qua prope ego EGEBRCTVS. regali fretuſ digni
tate cupio fideliſ inſ fideleſ inueniri. eʒ fidelium particepſ in regno celorum tantiſ apłiſ inter
dentibuſ effici deſiderans. Omnipotenti deo ſpecialiter concedo quandam portionem de tra
quam pſeceſſoreſ mei atʒ propinqui iure hereditario michi poſſidendam reliquint. ſcilicet qn
decim manentium in loco qui ſolito ab incoliſ Aepeltvne appellatur. Et hanc portionem largiar
aduenſ monaſterium eʒ ad ecclam eorundem beatorum aptorum ſetri eʒ pauli in Wyntonia ci
uitate. ad uſum familie que pro totiuſ xpiani popli ſalute xpo nubi deuota deſeruit. hanc
quippe tellurem fideliſſimuſ quidam pfectorum meorum uocabulo biuhþrharduſ olim me
donante poſſedit. ſed ille poſt modum ſine liberiſ defunctuſ. eandem terram ſine hereditaria

23. *Chartulary of Winchester Cathedral priory,*
grant by King Egbert to the Winchester community.

in the design. The charter relates to the appropriation of the parish church of Edlesborough in Buckinghamshire by St Albans Abbey in 1389. From the twelfth century onwards, it was not uncommon for a baron or bishop to give local churches into the care of the monasteries, replacing the rector with a vicar and enabling the monks to enjoy the greater part of the fruits whilst supervising church affairs. Monasteries came to demand such transfers of benefices and would obtain in advance a papal bull of authorization to forestall any possible objections.

Charters were the basic title deeds and records of privilege of monastic houses, but because of the difficulty of preserving individual scraps of parchment, often with bulky seals attached, their texts might be copied into books or rolls known as char-tularies for reference and use as evidence. The degree of elaboration of these manuscripts and scrupulousness of their scribes in copying accurately and recording only genuine documents, varied at different times and in different communities. The Sherborne Chartulary (exhibit 49), which is not a typical example, has been discussed above. The earliest surviving chartulary from a religious house in Britain is contained in folios 1–118 of exhibit 56. Compiled at Worcester in the early eleventh century, it consists of copies of deeds relating to the house arranged by counties, followed by copies of leases and some miscellaneous material.

Bound together with this is 'Hemming's Chartulary', another early compilation from Worcester, c.1090–1100. It is named after the monk Hemming who declares his identity and purpose on folio 131b; the charters are arranged by subject matter in four sections, preceded by a preface and an account of lost possessions. Most chartularies were functional and unremarkable in presentation, but particular care was lavished upon exhibit 57, which was written between 1130 and 1150 at the Old Minster, Winchester. In an attempt to imitate the appearance of the solemn charter, the docu-ments were copied in bookhand with large headings and decorated initials, the Anglo-Saxon version following the Latin in each case. [23], for example, shows a charter of King Egbert granting part of his lands at Aetheltune to the community at Winchester in 826.

If its service of the Lord was to be effective, the Benedictine monastery had to maintain its status in an increasingly competitive secular world. A monk's education must therefore extend beyond book-learning and contemplation to the realities of contemporary life, to administration and economy, to agriculture and business. The attitudes implanted in him from the beginning of his noviciate helped him to accept all duties, congenial and uncongenial, as part of a training directed to the glory of God, for whose sake he must learn to give of his best in whatever field he might be called to serve.

D. H. Turner

'THE WORK OF GOD'

N the idiom of the time St Benedict used the term 'the work of God', in Latin 'opus dei', for the liturgy, that is, the official prayer of the church. He devoted twelve chapters of his rule to those parts of it which were to be performed daily by his monks. It is noteworthy that he does not concern himself with the central act of the liturgy, namely the eucharist or mass. The daily solemn 'morning' or 'chapter' mass, high mass, and private masses in Benedictine and other religious houses were later developments. In St Benedict's time a single celebration of mass for a congregation on Sundays, feast-days, and other important occasions, which included special needs, was the custom. The daily services which St Benedict felt required organization were those known as the canonical hours, because of their allocation to particular times throughout the twenty-four hours of the day and night. They are, with their modern names, matins, lauds, prime, terce, sext, none, vespers, and compline, which together make up what is called the divine office. Matins was considered a night-time devotion and of the other hours lauds and vespers were regarded as more important. St Benedict's prescriptions for the canonical hours remained in honour amongst Benedictines until the liturgical reforms which followed the Second Vatican Council. They also gave the canonical hours as recited by Benedictines and others who followed their traditions — such as the Cistercians — features distinguishing them from the canonical hours as recited by 'non-Benedictines' in the western church. For example, in the Benedictine, or 'monastic', use matins on Sundays and greater festivals had twelve lessons, in the 'secular' use nine; vespers had four psalms, as against the five at 'secular' vespers; and the Nunc Dimittis which was such a feature of 'secular' compline was not employed in 'monastic' compline.

St Benedict's scheme of eight canonical hours received considerable accretions. Many of these were due to St Benedict of Aniane and Benedictine liturgical life reached its greatest elaboration in the Cluniac congregation, where in the eleventh century scarcely an hour's free time might remain over from the celebration of the liturgy and the necessities of life, such as eating and sleeping. The Regularis Concordia and Lanfranc's Constitutions envisage a less arduous existence. Nevertheless, the liturgical life of a Benedictine monk or nun in the high Middle Ages was demanding and involved. There were attempts in the thirteenth century and later, down to the Reformation, to curtail it, but they seem to have had little success. It must be emphasized that it is impossible to give a unified picture of the Benedictine 'opus dei' in the Middle Ages, or of medieval liturgy at all. The permutations and variations at different times of the year and as a result of the occurrence, and concurrence, of Sundays, feast-days and fast-days, of varying rank, were innumerable, whilst the disunity of the Benedictine order, and of the medieval church, increases the complexity. Only a generalized view can be sketched, drawing largely on sources preserved by the accidents of fate. In the picture the least certain element is the time-table. Lanfranc's Monastic Constitutions, for example, give no references to clock-time.

The principal additions to St Benedict's original cursus were: 1. The chapter office, a daily meeting of the community, the function of which was a mixture of devotions and business. It included readings from the martyrology and the rule of St Benedict and was usually held immediately before or after the 'morning' or 'chapter' mass, the first of the two daily conventual masses. 2. The trina oratio, a threefold devotion performed thrice daily: according to the Regularis Concordia, before matins, before prime in summer or terce in winter, and after compline. 3. The gradual psalms, namely psalms cxix-cxxxiii. 4. The penitential psalms, namely psalms vi, xxxi, xxxvii, l, ci, cxxix, and cxlii. 5. The litany of the saints. Many of the saints invoked were generally venerated throughout the western church, others were of local importance. The local names in litanies are valuable for the localization of liturgical books. 6. The psalmi familiares, intercessions for the king, queen, benefactors, and friends. 7. The suffrages, recited at the end of lauds and vespers. Again, the series generally includes references to saints of local importance. 8. The office of the dead, comprising only vespers, matins, and lauds. It was usually omitted on Sundays, greater festivals, and the last three days of holy week. 9. The office of all saints, comprising only vespers and lauds. 10. The office of the Blessed Virgin Mary. The last three items were modelled on the canonical hours, although only the office of the Virgin had the full eight hours. 11. The anthem of the Virgin Mary, commonly recited after compline and sometimes after other services. To this list should be added processions, which were a frequent feature of the medieval liturgy generally.

Benedictines have become famed for dignified performance of the liturgy, with impressive ceremonial and music. The amount of music and ceremony varies with the importance of a particular day and the resources of a particular house. In medieval Britain, at the larger monasteries on greater festivals probably all the divine office, part of the office of the Virgin, and the two conventual masses would be sung and there would be singing at processions. Otherwise, some of the items mentioned in the last paragraph were probably always said, privately as it were, although the normal place for their performance would be in the choir. Most of the others were probably never more than recited in monotone and, generally, what might be sung, but was not, was monotoned, although things like private masses would be said throughout. The traditional way of singing the liturgy was the monodic chanting known as plainsong, in the development of which Benedictines undoubtedly played a vital role. The

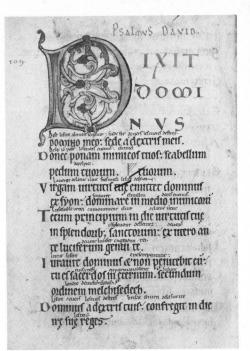

24. *St Albans Abbey: the choir. Watercolour by C. A. Buckler.*

25. *Psalter, the beginning of psalm cix.*

bulk of the repertoire of the so-called Gregorian chant, as it survives, was probably elaborated in the Franco-German lands, particularly in the monasteries there, *c.*750–850. The tenth-century monastic reformers in England drew on the riches of the Continent. St Ethelwold obtained expert singers from the monastery of Corbie, in France, to teach his monks, whilst St Dunstan appears to have been a musician himself, as well as an expert scribe and painter. He is credited with a setting of the Kyrie, known as 'Rex Splendens', and it has been conjectured that he may have perfected his artistic skills whilst in exile, at the monastery of St Peter, Ghent. Polyphony was far from spurned by the medieval Benedictines. For instance, the fourteenth-century customary of St Augustine's Abbey, Canterbury (exhibit 16), speaks of a two-part rendering of the sequence, the Benedictus and the Magnificat on greater festivals. Exhibit 25, an ordinal of Bury St Edmunds Abbey of the same period, several times mentions polyphonic settings of parts of the mass and the office. Whilst monks and nuns were expected to be familiar with plainsong, they were not necessarily experts at polyphony. In 1423 John Whethamstede, abbot of St Albans 1420–1440 and 1451–1465, a picture of whom is on the cover of this book, ordained that as his community could not provide satisfactory singers of polyphony from its own ranks, at least two professionals should be hired to sing at the mass of the Virgin and at vespers and high mass in choir on Sundays and feast-days. The use of organs was another thing which owed its diffusion to the reformers of the tenth century. Both Dunstan and Ethelwold are said to have built organs with their own hands and

Wulfstan (d. 963), precentor of Winchester Cathedral, has left an account of the remarkable organ installed there by Alphege, bishop of Winchester c.934–951. Its sound could be heard throughout the town and its reverberations could cause people to cover their ears.

The lii chapter of St Benedict's rule is on the oratory of the monastery, which is to be what it is called, a place of prayer, with nothing else done or kept there. It seems a long way from the primitive chapel at Monte Cassino to the great Benedictine churches which are monuments of architecture in Europe and elsewhere, and the many activities which have gone on in them. The heart of a Benedictine church is always the choir, where a monk or nun has his or her main place and where the monastic liturgy proper is performed. Exhibit 40 [**24**], a watercolour by C.A. Buckler (d. 1905) of the choir at St Albans, serves as an illustration of the centre of Benedictine life.

The principal source for the liturgy is the Bible. From it were taken in particular the psalms which were part of each of the hours and so widely used besides, and readings, very short ones called chapters at the day hours, longer ones at matins, and, of course, the epistle and gospel at mass. In any case, a Bible is an obvious possession for the full Christian life. The production of large, finely decorated, manuscripts of the Bible was a feature of the Romanesque period and a number survive of British provenance definitely connected with Benedictine monasteries. There is the Bible commissioned for Prior Talbot of Bury St Edmunds by his brother Hervey, the sacrist there, and illuminated by Master Hugo, a secular artist, between 1130 and 1140; there is the mid-twelfth-century Dover Bible from Christ Church, Canterbury; there is the Winchester Bible, c.1150–1180; there is the bible given to Durham Cathedral priory by Hugh de Puiset, bishop of Durham 1153–1195; and there is the Lambeth Bible (exhibit 95).

Not all big and beautiful bibles were for use in church. Some were for reading from during meals in the refectory and the Winchester Bible was probably one of these. The Lambeth Bible was very likely made for St Augustine's Abbey, Canterbury. Whether its writer and/or illuminator were Benedictine monks will almost certainly never be known, but it is known that the illuminator decorated a manuscript of the gospels for Wedric, abbot of the Benedictine house of Liessies, in Hainault, which was written by one John in 1146. The stylistic evidence indicates that the illuminator was an Englishman and the figural work in the Lambeth Bible makes it one of the masterpieces of English Romanesque, and indeed of Romanesque art anywhere, and of linearism of any time and place.

This can be superbly seen in the minature of the Tree of Jesse [**col. I**], which illustrates Isaiah's prophecy of Christ: 'there shall come forth a rod out of the stem of Jesse, and a branch shall grow out of his roots'. The picture is a symphony of line, dominated by the elongated figure of the Virgin Mary, posed centrally against a tree which grows out of the loins of a reclining Jesse. Drapery is completely turned into patterning and the Virgin and the half-length Christ above her are the only tranquil elements in a vortex of movement and expression.

Codification of the liturgy proceeded slowly, responding to the centralization of the western church and its religious orders. One of the earliest compilations to emerge was the psalter. St Benedict had been anxious that all the hundred and fifty psalms should be gone through in the divine office each week and apportioned them accordingly in his rule. The 'secular' use had a similar allocation. Monks and nuns were expected to know the psalms by heart and copies of them probably appeared first for use by dignitaries. Psalters became popular with all literate and pious people and were frequently embellished to a greater or lesser degree.

Besides the psalms, a medieval psalter normally has other contents, including a calendar, canticles, creeds, a litany of the saints, and various devotions, in particular the offices of the Virgin and the dead. Canticles are other songs of prayer from scripture employed in the liturgy, of which the 'Benedictus' at lauds and the 'Magnificat' at vespers are well known. An extremely fine psalter associated with a Benedictine prelate is exhibit 48, described in chapter 2. In chapter 1 mention has been made of another illuminated psalter with Benedictine connexions, exhibit 3. Two less splendid psalters have also been included in the exhibition, exhibits 23 and 38. The first of these, which has an interlinear French translation accompanying most of its text, was, on the evidence of its litany, originally executed for, and probably at, Peterborough Abbey in the late twelfth century. It seems quickly to have migrated to Crowland Abbey, since it is prefixed by a contemporary calendar of that house. It has no figural illumination, but some decorated initials. The 'D' at the beginning of psalm cix, the first psalm at vespers on Sunday, is illustrated here [25]. Exhibit 38, again of the twelfth century, has been assigned to Muchelney Abbey, because of its calendar and litany.

A calendar is indispensable for determining the day's services and is therefore widely found in liturgical books. Whilst its foundations are commemorations common throughout the church, it also contains others proper to particular places, and even persons. It provides the chief internal evidence for localizing a liturgical book, or any other in which it occurs, and on this localization may depend that of several other manuscripts related by script or decoration. A whole school of illumination may be constructed on liturgical localizations, principally from calendars. A calendar in a not obviously liturgical book is exhibit 24 [26]. Here a calendar of the use of Ely Cathedral priory is prefixed to a copy of the four gospels and the psalms, the whole dating from the thirteenth century. Finding the provenance of the calendar is helped because most of the notices in it have indications of liturgical rank, which is not always the case. The two highest ranks here are 'in cappis' and 'in albis'. The second designation refers to the ceremonial wearing of albs in choir by members of the community on the days in question, the first to the wearing of both albs and copes. The local feasts 'in copes' are those of St Etheldreda, the foundress of Ely, her Translation and its Octave day, her sisters Withburga, who has two feasts, and Sexburga, her niece Ermenilda, the Translation of St Benedict, Edmund, the martyred king of the East Anglia, and the Commemoration of St Alban. Ely legend had it that the genuine relics of Britain's protomartyr were brought there by Fritheric, the last Anglo-Saxon abbot of St Albans when he fled to join the resistance against William the Conqueror. Ely, therefore, kept this special feast of Alban.

The church's long history has, of course, enriched each day with the memory of many more than one worthy. A calendar is concerned with those who have a

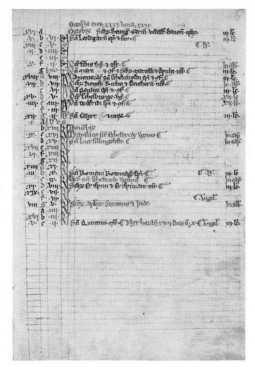

26. *Calendar of Ely Cathedral priory, the month of October.*

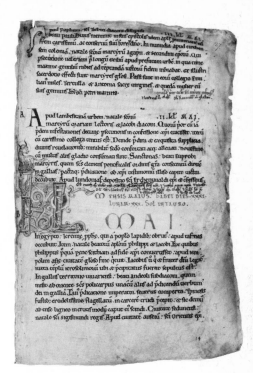

27. *Martyrology of St Augustine's Abbey, Canterbury, the end of the month of April and the beginning of May.*

liturgical cult. An attempt at a catalogue of some at least of each day's saints is provided by the martyrology, which is so called because originally it listed only those who had been killed for the faith. The Capitula of Aachen refer to the daily reading from the martyrology in the chapter office and it is a reminder of the days before the media that the passage read was always that about the following day. Exhibit 26 [27] is a twelfth-century martyrology from St Augustine's Abbey, Canterbury, which has historiated initials containing zodiacal figures for each month. The manuscript was unfortunately damaged in the fire of the Cottonian library in 1731. Added to the notices in the martyrology are obits of monks of St Augustine's and others for whom it was felt especially bounden to pray. The entries include, on 14th October, 'Harold, king of the English, and very many of our brethren', for St Augustine's took an active part in the Battle of Hastings.

The various parts of the divine office were in time put together in a book known as a breviary. Breviaries originated probably in the interests of clergy when travelling and the earlier ones therefore often contained texts for the mass and other services. Such is the case with the earliest surviving English monastic breviary, which comes from Winchcombe Abbey in the twelfth century and is now in the Bibliothèque Municipale at Valenciennes. There are four breviaries in the exhibition, exhibits 28, 29, 30, and 37. Exhibit 29 was executed possibly at Durham Cathedral priory *c.*1270

er la nunbre eft ances ves viols. le quatre solum ce la seonde ore v sa nege
se la quie seruir qui est la concon. e la pente eft apt la miise le vie sel un
cel miise ances qui est la concon. e vs seres en le seonide aed pnes le miise
espir ofi e bas en le seraftre angles a simil drst en pmes e en si de quues oele
schit les quatre oefles qui passe faft divesces conuecer ol pmes e for a sin
go se uil conuence a mui e termino a mui a pes ome les vies se sunt pou
ances mui sunt a cuites comunenadmit a mui vu pui pseut us pardu syu
sytante e sac vs vns aplus cost be ol due la concon ducec mous cel vie len sy
prue.

for use at its daughter house at Coldingham. Whilst its contents have been more or less sorted into place, the hymns, which are accompanied by music, and the canticles for matins remain as entities by themselves. The Coldingham Breviary contains one miniature [28], of a monk kneeling before the Virgin and Child. In 1521 the manuscript was given by Hugh Whitehead, the last prior (1519–1540) and first dean (1541–1551) of Durham, to Richard Crosby, one of his monks. Exhibit 29 is a Cluniac breviary and missal, c.1300. Masses are given for only the more important days and the nature of its contents together with its small size propose it at once as a travelling companion. The liturgical indications are that it was for a superior in the English group of Cluniac monasteries which depended on the French mother house of La Charité-sur-Loire. Exhibit 28 is the first volume of a two-volume breviary of Muchelney Abbey, written in the late thirteenth century. It has no eucharistic material, but contains copious additions by way of memoranda down to the sixteenth century relating mainly to Muchelney's spiritual and temporal affairs. The scope and relevance of the notes suggest that the breviary was for the use of the abbots of Muchelney. Exhibit 37 [29] is an approximate example of how the breviary finally developed. It is of the liturgical use of St Albans, and was printed c.1526 on the press run in the abbey precincts by the layman John Herford.

Material supplementary to the original divine office is sometimes found in breviaries, but often appears in a separate compilation, the book of hours, the principal item in which is the office of the Virgin. Books of hours became very popular with secular clergy and the laity, not least women, replacing the psalter as the standard book of devotion. Although they have come customarily to be regarded as books designed, frequently with lavish ornamentation, for layfolk, this was never their *raison d'être*. Several survive, some finely illuminated, which were made for ecclesiatics, including Benedictines. Exhibit 39 is an example of a simple book of hours, without illumination, of the use of Durham Cathedral priory. Towards the beginning it has a list of obits to be kept there, the most recent name in which is that of King Richard III (1485).

The counterpart to the breviary is the missal, containing everything necessary for the celebration of the eucharist. Its foundation is the sacramentary, a book containing the prayers used at mass and some other rites. The oldest surviving sacramentary of probable English origin is the earliest part of the Leofric Missal (exhibit 32). The manuscript takes its name from its sometime owner, Leofric, the first bishop of Exeter (d. 1072), who gave it to his cathedral. Its earliest part dates from the early years of the tenth century and it was once thought to have been written in the diocese of Arras or of Cambrai, in France. But while the scribe, who was probably also the illuminator [30], is clearly of continental origin, the texts in the sacramentary, in particular those for a coronation service, point towards execution in England. A calendar of Glastonbury Abbey and other material were added to the sacramentary c.970 and some more additions were made in the eleventh century. It seems likely that the sacramentary was at Glastonbury when it received the calendar and that it was

◀ *28. Breviary of Coldingham priory, the Virgin and Child.*

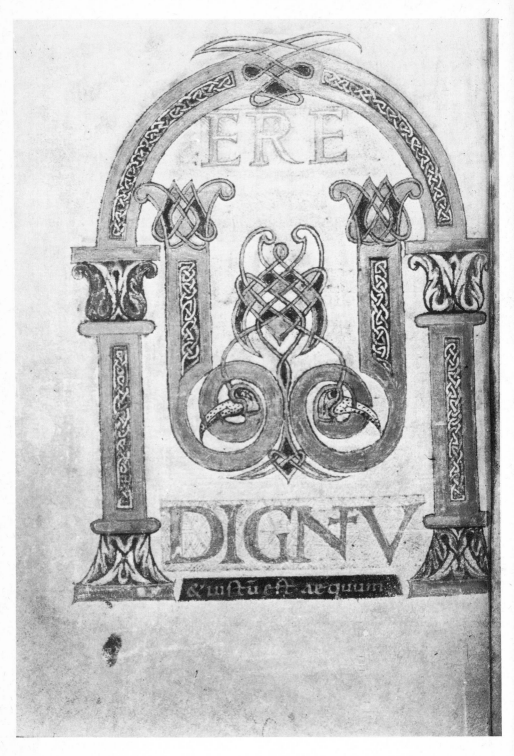

30. *The Leofric Missal, the beginning of the canon of the mass.*

29. Breviary of St Albans Abbey, the beginning of the psalter.

written probably in the south-west of England, if not at Glastonbury. It witnesses to the introduction of continental models into England in the tenth century and it may have been at sometime in the hand of St Dunstan himself. The original ornamentation, which is solely decorative, is in the Franco-Saxon style of Carolingian art; some drawings were done in connexion with the calendar, including a figure symbolic of life and another symbolic of death. The earliest surviving complete English missal — complete, that is, in what it contains, for the first part of the manuscript is missing — is in the Bibliothèque Municipale at Le Havre and was written for, and presumably at, the monastery of the New Minster, Winchester, in the second half of the eleventh century. The choral parts of the mass in it are accompanied by music, a phenomenon which also occurs sometimes in breviaries. The reason for this is obscure. There seems never to have been any tradition of an unaccompanied officiant singing the choral texts at mass or the office.

A later missal is exhibit 43 [31], a well-thumbed example from the fourteenth century and of the use of Durham Cathedral priory. It was given to the altar of Sts John the Baptist and Margaret, one of the altars in the famous chapel of the nine altars at the east end of Durham Cathedral, by a Prior John of Durham. He cannot be exactly identified: there are a number of Johns who ruled at Durham in the material period.

Sacramentary, lectionaries for the gospels and epistles, and the textual parts at least of choir books: these were the principle ingredients of a missal. The choirbooks containing the plainsong settings for the mass have come to be known as graduals, whilst those with the settings for the office are antiphonals, antiphonaries, or antiphoners — three terms which were earlier used for the collections of chants both for the mass and

D. H. Turner

'GUESTS, WHO ARE NEVER LACKING IN A MONASTERY'

THE development of Benedictine houses into centres of civilization drew to them not only aspirants for the religious life, but many and divers persons desirous of sharing in various ways in the benefits accruing to that life. Despite the independence of each Benedictine house, the Benedictine family has always been large, with monasteries entering into associations with other houses and with outside individuals, both lay and ecclesiastic. Benedictines have a noble reputation for hospitality, encouraged by their founder himself. The liii chapter of his rule is on receiving guests and the lxvi on the porter of the monastery, who is to be a wise old man, who knows how to give and how to receive an answer. Guests are to be received as Christ himself, with special care shown to the poor and strangers: 'For the very fear men have of the rich procures them honour'. The kitchen for the abbot and guests is to be apart by itself, 'so that guests, who are never lacking in a monastery, may not disturb the brethren by coming at unlooked-for hours'. In the interests of hospitality the superior may break his fast, except on a principal fast-day; and during the greater silence, at night after compline, when a Benedictine should normally never speak, he or she may do so if the presence of guests requires. Chapter lvi of St Benedict's rule, on the table of the abbot, says this is to be always with the guests and strangers. 'But as often as there are few guests, it shall be in his power to invite any of the brethren'.

The provisions of chapter lvi were obviously designed to reconcile hospitality with protection of the religious community itself from the irruption of the world. Nevertheless, it became the basis for one far from desirable development, namely the separation of the abbot from his community, whereby he became a corporation sole with his own establishment. Reformers early noticed this danger. The Capitula of Aachen reverse St Benedict's regulations and envisage guests eating in the refectory. The Regularis Concordia sternly forbids the abbot or any of the brethren to eat outside the refectory, except in case of sickness. Both it and even more Lanfranc's Monastic Constitutions imply that ordinary guests would be given their food in the guest-house. Lanfranc expressly states that visiting clerics could be granted permission to join the monks in the refectory. However, the twelfth century saw the abbot's household recognized as an independent part of a monastery, although only favoured guests would be invited to his table.

Nevertheless, as abbots became more and more great lords, their liabilities for entertainment became no light burden. Royalty frequently visited the great abbeys, like St Albans and Bury St Edmunds, and even held parliaments there. In 1423 the king's uncle, Humphrey, duke of Gloucester, and Jacqueline, his duchess, accompanied by three hundred retainers, kept Christmas at St Albans. A similar number of people attended Gloucester's brother and sister-in-law, John, duke of Bedford, and his wife Anne, when they came in 1426. The king himself, Henry VI, was at St Albans three times in 1459, first for Easter — 25th March that year — until 18th April; second for the feast of St Alban (22nd June), when he stayed six days; and third for the feast of the Decollation of St John the Baptist (29th August), when he remained for nearly six weeks. On the occasion of the Easter visit he was received into confraternity, together with two hundred and twenty other people. In 1433–1434, as a boy of twelve, Henry was at Bury St Edmunds from Christmas to St George's Day (23rd April) and was received into confraternity there at the close of his stay. In preparation for the visit, William Curteys, abbot of Bury from 1429 to 1446, employed eighty workmen for a month on renovating the abbot's residence. In com-

35. *The New Minster Liber Vitae, the blessed and the damned.*

36. *Durham Cathedral. Drawing by J. Buckler.*

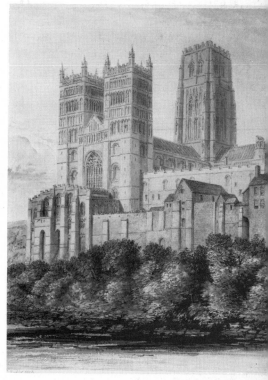

memoration of it he had the poet Lydgate, one of his monks, put together a verse life of St Edmund. Exhibit 71 is the actual copy of this given to the king. It contains one hundred and twenty miniatures, one of which shows the king praying before St Edmund's shrine [col. III], and another shows him receiving the book.

Confraternity, both individual and corporate, was formal association with a religious community, not necessarily a Benedictine one. Corporate confraternity could be very complete. Evesham Abbey had agreements with the monasteries of Malmesbury, Whitby, St Mary's, York, and Odensee in Denmark whereby monks of any of these houses had rights when at any of the others, as if they were members of that house. St Augustine's, Canterbury, had a similar relationship with its parent foundation by St Gregory the Great, St Andrew's, Rome. Such plurality of stability was forbidden by the Fourth Lateran Council in 1215. For a layman or an ecclesiastic, individual confraternity might lead to monastic profession when dying and burial in the monastic habit. More generally confraternity meant remembrance in the prayers, for the living and the dead, of a monastery.

Monasteries kept 'books of life', in Latin 'libri vitae', recording the names of their members, benefactors, and associates — and associations. Such are exhibits 66, 67 and 68. Exhibit 66 is the Liber Vitae of the monastery of the New Minster, Winchester, originally written probably in 1031 by Aelsine, a monk of the house. It has additions down to the sixteenth century, by which time the community had moved to a new site in 1110, becoming Hyde Abbey. Some of the names in the book were to be read out each day by the subdeacon at high mass and after the offertory the book was placed on the altar. At the beginning of the manuscript are two illustrations in tinted outline. The first shows King Canute and his wife, Elfgifu, presenting a gold cross to the New Minster, the second, spread over two pages (the right hand one is reproduced as [35]), the fates of the blessed and the damned. Exhibit 67, the Liber Vitae of Durham Cathedral priory, is very well travelled. It was begun at Lindisfarne in the mid-ninth century and, like exhibit 66, it has continuations down to the sixteenth century. Lindisfarne was founded in 635 as a monastery in the Celtic tradition. In 875 the community fled before the Vikings, taking with them their treasures and relics, including the body of St Cuthbert, the Lindisfarne Gospels, and their Book of Life. From 883 to 995 they were at Chester-le-Street, removing to Durham in 995, thus establishing the see of Durham. By the Norman Conquest the community had become in effect secularized. In 1083 the Norman William of St Carilef, bishop of Durham 1081–1096, himself a Benedictine monk, replaced seculars with Benedictines in the service of his cathedral [36].

COLOUR PLATES

I. The Lambeth Bible, vol. i, the Tree of Jesse.

III. John Lydgate, Life of St Edmund, *Henry VI before the saint's shrine.*

II. The Benedictional of St Ethelwold, St Benedict.

IV. Matthew Paris, Historia Anglorum, *the Virgin and Child.*

SCS
BE   NE
DIC   TUS

AB   BI

O alle men present / or in absence
Which to seynt Edmund haue deuocion
With hool herte / and deth reuerence
Seyn this Antephne / and this Orison
Two hundred daies / ys grauntid off pardon
Write and registred / asseen his hooly shryne
Which for our feith / suffrede passion
Blyssyd Edmund / kyng / martir / and virgyne

O felicia oscula Lactentis labis impressa. cu
inter crebra iudicia reptauit inf... ncie
utpare ber̄ er te fili mei Alluder cu
neuiuf er patre d̄r d̄i geniꝰ imparer

RATMATHIAS: PARISIENS

A lavish Liber Vitae is the Golden Book of St Albans (exhibit 68). It was compiled in 1380, apparently on the instructions of the abbot, Thomas de la Mare, in order to collect in one volume names previously inscribed on various rolls kept at various altars. The author was the St Albans monk and historian Thomas Walsingham, at the time precentor, and therefore head of the scriptorium. The monk William de Wyllum wrote out the book, but a layman, Alan Strayler, illustrated it with numerous representations of people mentioned in it [37], including his own portrait. He made a present to the abbey of the price of the paints used in illuminating the manuscript, namely 3s 4d. The finished book was to lie on the high altar of St Albans and all those recorded in it were to share fully in the spiritual benefits of the monastery, which included three sung masses each day, that is, the morning mass, a mass of the Virgin, and the high mass; at least three said masses, one of the Virgin for the church, one of St Alban for benefactors, and one for the dead; and nine years and one hundred and seventy days' indulgences. The manuscript has additions, both written and illustrated (front cover), down to the sixteenth century. A fascination of its miniatures is that the figures in them are shown with representations of gifts they made to St Albans. Thomas of Hatfield, bishop of Durham (d. 1381) appears with the mazer which he gave to the community, 'which we call Wassail'; Lady Petronella de Benstede (d. 1342) holds a round portable altar of jasper set in silver, on which St Augustine of Canterbury was supposed to have celebrated mass; Agnes Paynel, nun of Sopwell, holds one of the set of black satin vestments, embroidered with her initials, 'A' and 'P', and stars, which she presented; and so on. Many of the figures hold charters or money-bags, whilst a more unfortunate benefactor is Walter de Amundesham, 'faithful steward of this church', who was slain by the tenants of St Albans, and is depicted meeting his end.

Not least amongst the attractions of a monastery for the public were the holy relics it preserved, especially when these included the remains of a saint who might work miracles. Pilgrims may have been a severe disturbance to the religious life, but they were also an important source of revenue and monasteries vied with each other — often unscrupulously — for the possession of relics which would draw the faithful. Some Benedictine houses were famous shrines, with Christ Church, Canterbury, with its relics of St Thomas Becket, eclipsing all. Others worth mention are Bury St Edmunds; Crowland, which had the body of St Guthlac; Durham, with relics of St Cuthbert and the Venerable Bede; Ely, with relics of St Etheldreda; Glastonbury; St Albans; and Westminster, with relics of St Edward the Confessor.

Glastonbury is steeped in legend. St Joseph of Arimathea was supposed to have brought thither the Holy Grail. A monastery was supposed to have been founded there by St Patrick and its church consecrated by a visitation to earth of Jesus Christ himself. In that church King Arthur was thought to have been buried. Exhibit 70 is a fourteenth-century list of relics at Glastonbury Abbey [38]. These include shrines of St Dunstan, St Patrick, his disciple St Benignus, and St David. Dunstan's relics are said to be a gift from King Edmund Ironside (1016) and several other relics are stated to have been given by King Edmund 'the elder' (d. 946). St David's relics were brought from Wales in the time of King Edgar 'by a certain matron Elswytha'. Glastonbury's claims about their sacred holdings were far from undisputed. Christ

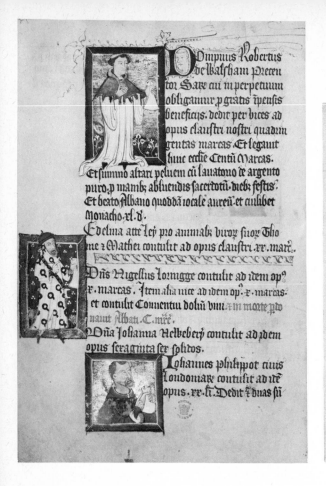

Church, Canterbury, for instance, were firmly convinced that they retained St Dunstan's body.

Short of a certifiable miracle, pilgrims expected some benefits from their journeyings. This was formalized in the doctrine of indulgences, based on the belief that even though a sinner were reconciled with God and absolved, there was still a penalty to be paid, in this life or the next, which could be remitted by the church, drawing on the 'treasury of merits' accumulated by Christ and the saints. To obtain an indulgence the faithful had to perform certain pious duties and the indulgence could be complete, that is, 'plenary', or partial, reckoned as so many days or years, being a remission of the penalty which would have been expiated by the performance of penance for that time on earth. It is small wonder that Luther and other reformers have found this computistical approach to divine mercy objectionable. If an establishment could offer indulgences to its guests, it became that much more popular. Exhibits 82 and 83 are letters of indulgence in favour of Reading Abbey which was in a good position to expect visitors because of its situation on a principal highway. In exhibit 82 Becket's future enemy Gilbert Foliot, when bishop of Hereford (1147–1163), grants twenty days' indulgence to all visiting Reading on the feast of St James (25th July), or during its octave. Reading claimed to have relics of the apostle.

Some indulgences can scarcely escape being labelled commercial transactions, especially those soliciting money for buildings and hawked around by pardoners. Exhibit 81 is a document appealing for the fabric fund of the small nunnery of King's

Far left

37. *The Golden Book of St Albans, accounts and miniatures of benefactors, including Robert Waltham, precentor of Salisbury, Sir Nigel Loring, K.G., and Sir John Philipot, mayor of London.*

Left

38. *List of relics at Glastonbury Abbey, page relating to the shrine of St Patrick.*

Below

39. *Pilgrim's sign, showing St Thomas Becket on horseback.*

40. St Albans Abbey: the interior during a procession. Watercolour by J. C. Buckler.

Mead, Derby, in the thirteenth century and detailing the benefits for donors, including one hundred and thirty days' indulgence. Donations could be given to the bearer of the document. Souvenirs were as popular in the Middle Ages as now. Exhibits 72–75 and 77–79 are badges, or 'signs', denoting the successful accomplishment of a pilgrimage. Exhibits 72, 73, 74 and 75 all related to Canterbury and Becket, exhibit 75 being a representation of the saint on horseback [39]. A matrix survives for the making of such a badge (exhibit 76).

A very full picture of the pilgrimage trade is to be found in the Customary of the Shrine of St Thomas Becket (exhibit 69). This was compiled in 1428 by John Vyel and Edmund Kyngyston, two monks of Christ Church, Canterbury, then guardians of the shrine. It is prefixed to a late thirteenth-century manuscript of two twelfth-century lives of the saint in French, the second of which, by Guernes de Pont-Sainte-Maxence, was apparently read out of this very book to the pilgrims who came for the feast of Becket on 29th December. The fifth jubilee of St Thomas had been celebrated in 1420 with a plenary indulgence for all who made the Canterbury pilgrimage for the feast of his Translation (7th July) or during the following fortnight. Now, a few years later, the observances connected with the shrine are set forth. The devotions performed there, the care of its treasures, the duties towards its visitors, the outgoings from its revenues, all are meticulously rehearsed. The customary has only recently become available and materially fills out information about one of the richest and most famous centres in Christendom, which Henry VIII destroyed in 1538. Sadly, no satisfactory graphic representation of Becket's shrine survives; exhibit 80 is an artist's impression of a reliquary being carried in procession, in which J.C. Buckler imagines a scene from the Middle Ages at St Albans Abbey [40].

The corporal works of mercy have not been neglected by Benedictines. The Regularis Concordia presumes the regular maintenance of a number of poor by a monastery and there is a famous description of the aid given to refugees by Ethelwig, abbot of Evesham 1058–1077, after William the Conqueror had pacified the west country. King Stephen's reign saw similar acts of charity by houses such as Christ Church, Canterbury, St Albans, and Abingdon. Some hospitals were founded by Benedictines, but they did not usually make themselves responsible for their upkeep. The opinion of an intelligent layman on the social obligations of the religious houses — although he was not speaking only of Benedictines — is expressed by Robert Aske, the leader of the 'Pilgrimage of Grace' of 1536. 'He did grudge . . . because the abbeys in the north parts gave great alms to poor men and laudably served God . . . And by occasion of the said suppression the divine service of almighty God is much minished . . . the temple of God ruined, the ornaments and relics of the church of God unreverent used, the tombs and sepulchres of honourable and noble men pulled down and sold, none hospitality now in these places kept . . . Also divers and many of the said abbeys were in the mountains and desert places, where the people be rude of conditions and not well taught the law of God, and when the said abbeys stood, the said people had not only worldly refreshing in their bodies but also spiritual refuge . . . for none was in these parts denied, neither horsemeat nor mansmeat . . . also all gentlemen were much succoured in their needs with money; their young sons there succoured, and in nunneries their daughters brought up in virtue'.

Rachel Stockdale

BENEDICTINE LIBRARIES AND WRITERS

OOKS and architecture are the visible legacy of the medieval Benedictines in Britain. The modern layman who seeks a point of contact with the cultural spirit of the black monks may turn to the remains of the churches which they built, or to the manuscripts which they copied and illuminated, and the history and literature which they wrote. Since books are the *raison d'être* of the present exhibition, consideration must be given to those aspects of the Benedictine environment which inspired their composition and production.

Reading and spiritual exercises occupied about four hours a day in St Benedict's summer horarium, and these activities were equated with manual labour as useful ways of combating idleness, the enemy of the soul. It was assumed that all monks would be able to read, if not to write. The choice of reading matter was restricted in the early period to scripture and the church fathers, but the spiritual exercise of 'lectio divina' could also embrace meditation, learning by heart and preparation of liturgical offices, private prayer and even, since St Benedict made no separate provision for it, the copying and illuminating of manuscripts. Recognition of the intrinsic value of reading and writing came slowly in England, under the influence of the tenth-century reformers, the example of the Cluniacs, who devoted more time to study than to manual labour, and the inspiration of Lanfranc, who was probably responsible for the development at Canterbury of a scriptorium or writing school on the continental model. By the late thirteenth century, books were an accepted part of English Benedictine life. In contrast to the attitude prevailing two hundred years earlier, a General Chapter regulation of 1277 called for monks to 'study, write, correct, illuminate, and bind books according to their capacities, rather than labour in the fields.'

If monks were expected to read and copy, their monasteries must have possessed collections of books, but until the fifteenth century, there would be no single room set aside as a library. Books were functional and were kept in the part of the monastery where they were most often used; service-books in the church, books for reading aloud at mealtimes in the refectory, and books for private perusal, including some secular texts for the education of the young, in the cloister. The cantor or precentor seems generally to have assumed the role of librarian as an extension of his original duty to direct the music and care for the service-books. Some of the foremost monastic authors, such as Eadmer and William of Malmesbury occupied this post, proving that it was considered appropriate to monks of literary inclination.

Had it not been for the disruption of the Reformation, and the subsequent travels and loss of identity of those monastic books which survived, the libraries of medieval houses would have supplied valuable evidence about the life of their communities; the number of books and the richness of their execution reflecting the wealth of the establishments, their contents, the interests of the monks, the methods of acquisition, the zeal of individual abbots, and the exchanges between houses, the degree of intellectual contact. Modern scholars have attempted to identify the provenance of as many medieval manuscripts as possible, in the hopes of reconstructing, at least in outline, some of the monastic collections. The Benedictine cathedral priory of St Andrew at Rochester has proved one of the most fruitful fields of research, for over one hundred of its volumes have been identified in the British Library, and some thirty-seven elsewhere. In addition there are three library lists or catalogues extant, and a list of donations including many books, which can be used to form an assessment of the material that is lost.

Unlike other monasteries which were in effect under royal patronage, Rochester's patron was the archbishop of Canterbury, and thus it maintained specially close links with the greatest scriptorium and school of illumination in medieval England. The library was first developed under Ernulph (1114–1124), one of the Norman bishops who brought his learning from across the Channel, and an independent scriptorium evolved about the same time. Rochester was therefore not only acquiring but also producing books during a critical period of intellectual revival. By 1202, it possessed about three hundred volumes, compared with about six hundred at Christ Church, Canterbury c.1170. This figure had doubled by the Dissolution, when Durham, the greatest book-collector among the English monasteries, had amassed some three thousand volumes. Durham, however, has lost most of its stock since the sixteenth century, whereas an exceptionally high proportion of Rochester books, between a quarter and a fifth, survives. Credit in this respect is due to Henry VIII who, when he dissolved the monasteries, appropriated a selection of their books for his son's library, a collection which eventually passed almost intact to the British Museum. The particular attraction of Rochester books has never been explained. Henry was as eccentric in the monasteries he chose to plunder as in the subject matter of the volumes he selected to acquire. Virtually ignoring the richer pickings of St Augustine's, Canterbury, he seized upon Rochester, taking among other things, patristic texts and illuminated manuscripts which he generally rejected elsewhere.

The majority of surviving Rochester books have remained together and preserved their unity as a collection, but even more significant is the fact that most were already marked with the name of the house in an ex-libris inscription, enabling strays to be identified with certainty. The use of the ex-libris was unknown before the twelfth century, and even then it did not become widespread, although the larger Benedictine houses favoured it. The typical Rochester form was 'Liber de claustro Roffensi',

P

RE
VA
RI
CAT̄S
EST

AUTEM CΩOAB IN ISRŁ:
post quā mortuus est
achab. Ceciditq; ocho
zias p cancellos cenacu
li sui quod habebat in
samaria. & egrotauit.
Misitq; nuncios. dicens
ad eos. Ite consulite
beelzebub deum acha
ron: utrum uiuere
queam de infirmitate
mea hac. Angłs autē
dr̄i locutus est ad he
liam thesbiten dicens.
Surge & ascende in oc
cursum nuncioꝛ regl
samarie. & dices ad eos.
Hunquidnon ꝫ ds̄ in ī
rael. ut eatis ad consu
lendū beelzebub deū
acharon: Quamobrē

hec dicit dr̄s. De lectulo
sup quē ascendisti non descen
des. sed morte moueris.
Et abiit helias. Reuersiq; nunc
ti ad ochoziam. Qui dyxit
eis. Quare reuersi estis?
At illi responderūt ei. Uir
occurrit nobis. & dyxit
ad nos. Ite & reuertimini
ad regē qui misit uos. &
dicite ei. hec dicit dr̄s.
Hunquid non erat ds̄ in isrł
quia misisti ut consulatur
beelzebub ds̄ acharon:
Iccirco de lectulo sup quē
ascendisti non descendes.
sed morte moueris.Qui
dyxit eis. Cuius figure &
habitus est uir q̄ occurrit
uobis. & locutus est uerba
hec: At illi dyxerūt. Uir
pilosus. & zona pellicia
accinctus renib; Qui ait.
helias thesbites est. Misitq;
ad eum quinquagenariū
principem. & quinquagin
ta qui erant sub eo. Qui
ascendit ad eū. sedentiq;
in uertice montis ait. Ho
mo dei. rex precepit ut
descendas. Respondensq;

usually written at the foot of the fly-leaf or first folio, as in exhibit 97, and sometimes in juxtaposition with an anathema, cursing anyone who should steal, deface, or alter the book. All the exhibited items 96–103 have the ex-libris, except for the Rochester Bible (exhibit 101), whose provenance can be determined from its style of illustration. In the early twelfth century when this Bible was made, the script of Rochester was no more than a variant of that of Christ Church, and on palaeographical grounds alone, it might well have been prepared at Canterbury as a gift for the subordinate house. The decoration of the initials is, however, quite distinctive [41]. Although derived from the Canterbury school, comparison with other manuscripts known to have come from Rochester leaves no doubt that the Bible too was a local production. The thick, fleshy foliage, heavily shaded and contrasting with the thin animals which inhabit the bars of the letters, the solid figures and rich, dark colours may be compared with those in exhibit 98 [42] and in Royal MS. 5 D.i. A second Rochester style of illumination can be seen in exhibit 100 [43]. Although a companion volume to Royal MS. 5 D.i, it was produced at a later date and is characterized by pale colours, smaller, neater initials and interrelated figures.

42. *St Gregory the Great, Moralia on Job, from Rochester Cathedral priory. Beginning of book xxviii, initial P.*

◀ **41.** *The Rochester Bible, II Kings, initial P, with the Ascension of Elijah.*

43. *St Augustine,* Enarrationes super Psalmos, *from Rochester Cathedral priory.*

Not all the books in the Rochester library were copied in its own scriptorium; in fact, only one of the exhibited volumes (exhibit 97) claims unequivocally to have been written there and identifies its scribe: 'Liber beati augustini de Trinitate quem in eodem claustro (ie. Rochester) scripsit Humfridus precentor'. In this case, it would seem that the librarian copied material which was required, perhaps from an exemplar borrowed from Christ Church or another neighbouring house. Humfridus appears again in exhibit 96 in the inscription 'Memoriale Humfridi precentoris', the implication being that this was a personal possession, perhaps bequeathed to the priory on his death. Proper names in the genitive case (exhibits 99 and 100), or in the accusative with 'per' (exhibits 98, 102 and 103), both following the ex-libris inscription, are common in Rochester manuscripts. Their meaning is not entirely clear; the former seems to indicate ownership, the latter could mean that the book was commissioned, donated or even copied by the person named. Exhibit 103 is unlikely to have been produced at Rochester, as the illustrations are French in style. A note referring to the book's having been used as a pledge or security for a loan (exhibits 97 and 103) may give information as to its whereabouts at an earlier or later stage of its history.

The method of acquisition of a particular book was not of overwhelming concern to the monastic reader, unless it happened to be donated by an influential benefactor. The earliest library catalogues were in the form of lists of donations, and it was not until the twelfth century that experiments began with other kinds of classification. A tantalizing entry in Royal MS. 10 A. xii, f.111b records the volumes which Alexander, precentor of Rochester at the turn of the twelfth century, 'either wrote or

44. *St Augustine*, De Doctrina Christiana, etc., *library list of Rochester Cathedral priory.*

45. *Bestiary and Lapidary, from Rochester Cathedral priory, the unicorn.*

dicitur: propter incarnationis ei humilitate ipso
dicente. Discite a me quia mitis sum et humilis corde.
Similis est hedo unicornis: quia ipse saluator factus est
in similitudine carnis peccati· et de peccato dampna
uit peccatum. Vnicornis sepe cum elephantis certa
men habet· et in uentrem uulneratum prosternit·.

Incis dictus: quia in luporum genere numera
tur. Est enim bestia maculis distincta: ut pardus.
sed similis lupo. Huius urinam converti in duri
ciam preciosi lapidis dicunt dicunt qui ligurius
appellatur. Quod et ipsas linces sentire· uel docu
mento probatur. Nam egestum liquorem arenis

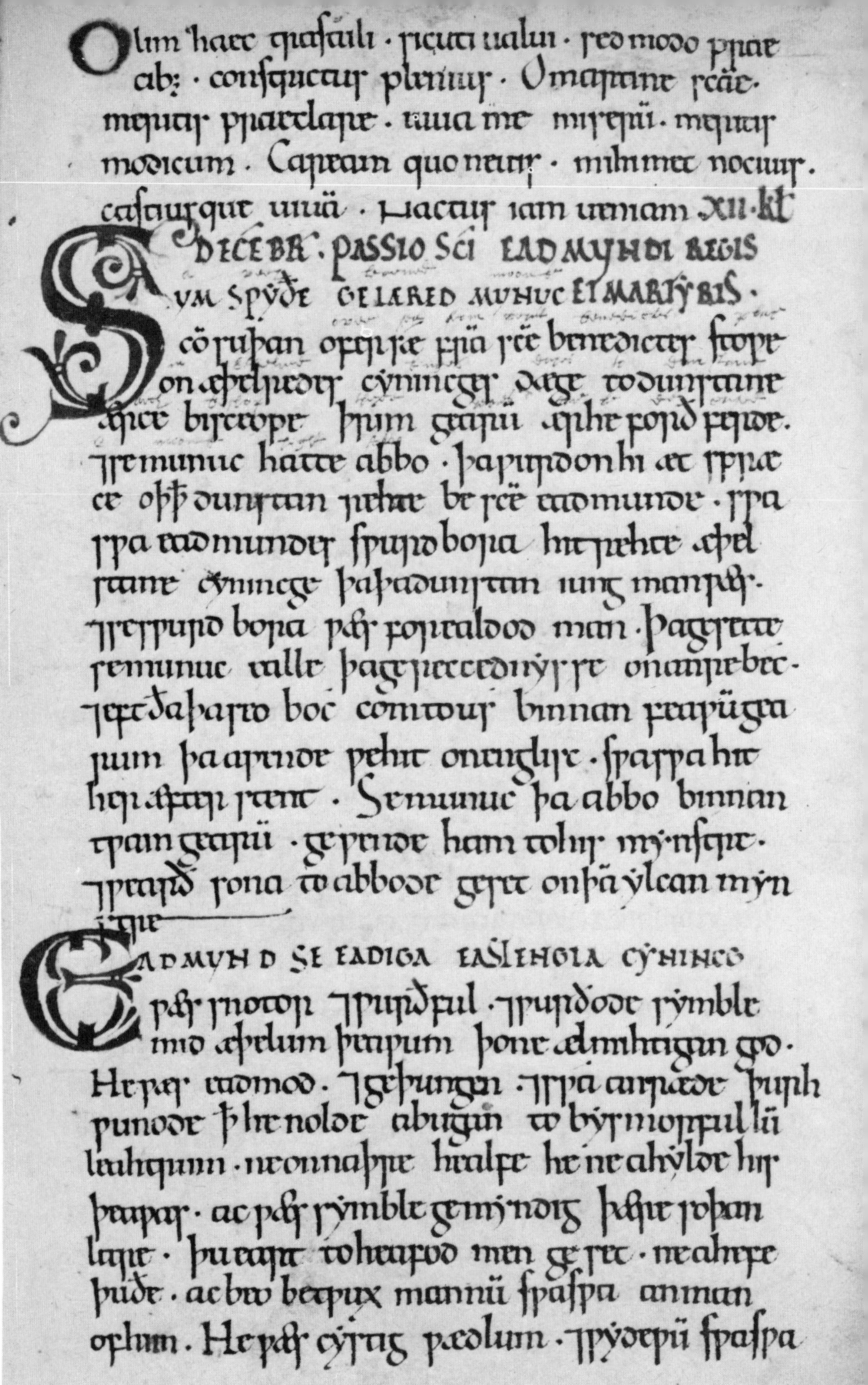

acquired' ('uel scripsit uel acquisiuit'), without specifying which. The first two items, part of an Old Testament and a complete Bible, he undoubtedly wrote, for the verb is 'scripsit'. Thereafter the verbs are omitted, rendering the meaning obscure. The contents of the volumes are in any case so vaguely described that comparison with the extant manuscripts or with the other lists is impossible. In contrast, Alexander himself compiled in 1202 a more scientific catalogue, which he had inserted on the fly-leaves of exhibit 96 [**44**]. It comprises two hundred and eighty volumes but must represent a larger number of individual works, because by convention if several were bound together in one volume, only the first would be mentioned. About half the extant manuscripts from Rochester in the Royal collection can be identified on this list. Alexander made a rudimentary attempt at classification. The first five sections are arranged under authors: St Augustine (twenty-three volumes), St Gregory (six volumes), St Ambrose (seven volumes), St Jerome (thirteen volumes) and Bede (five volumes). There follow the 'general library' (commune librarium), and the 'special collections' ('Aliud librarium in archa cantoris' and 'Librarium magistri Hamonis'). Twenty books were added without a heading after Alexander's name, and finally came the 'branch library', half a dozen books in the care of Robert, prior of Walton, a cell of Rochester near Felixstowe. A similar classification is found in a slightly earlier but fragmentary list included in the Textus Roffensis, which is in the Chapter Library at Rochester.

The conclusion to be drawn from the library lists and from the extant volumes is that in the Middle Ages Rochester must have had a fairly typical library for its size, in which most branches of learning were represented: scripture, liturgy, the fathers, scholastics and classics, literature, philosophy, grammar, logic, history, and science [**45**]. Religious texts, including commentaries and homilies, have survived in about equal numbers with the writings of the church fathers. History has fared nearly as well, but literature and science have virtually disappeared. The classics which were well represented in the 1202 list have survived in only five relatively obscure texts: Lucan, Solinus, in two copies, Statius and Juvenal. Few monastic libraries preserved any manuscripts from before the tenth century. Rochester's earliest survival is a tenth-century copy of Statius but the majority are of twelfth- and thirteenth-century date, and there are a few printed books. Most were in Latin, but two extant volumes of sermons in English should be noted. Exhibits 96–103 are a selection of Rochester manuscripts from the British Library's Royal collection, representative so far as is permitted by the accidents of preservation described above.

The monks who copied and illuminated manuscripts for their libraries were anonymous, unless by chance identified in an inscription or colophon, or associated with a particular style of drawing. The great names among the medieval Benedictines were those who engaged in creative writing, whether literary or historical. It is as authors, not as monks, that they are remembered, even though their work was invariably coloured by their experience of the cloister.

Experience of the tenth-century monastic revival, and in particular, contact with St Ethelwold who taught him as a young man at Winchester, were undoubtedly the inspiration of Aelfric (c.950–1020). To distinguish him from others of the same name, he usually bears the epithet 'The Grammarian', which testifies to one aspect of his talent.

Contemporaries knew him as an historian second only to Bede, and his opposition to the doctrine of transubstantiation earned him in the later Middle Ages an undeserved reputation as a theologian and controversialist. His real interests, however, were in education and monastic reform, the subjects of greatest concern to St Ethelwold himself. For the guidance of his fellow monks, and without any serious literary pretensions, Aelfric wrote pastoral letters, a paraphrase of the Old Testament, a grammar, and in later life when he became abbot of Eynsham, an abbreviation of the Regularis Concordia for domestic use. At the request of his literary patron Ethelmaer, he went in 987 to the newly refounded monastery of Cerne in Dorset as a teacher. There he began work on the Homilies or *Liber Sermonum Catholicorum Anglice,* the first two books of which were finished about 993 and 995 respectively. They consisted of conventional sermons, largely on doctrinal matters, for saints' days and Sundays, which Aelfric translated into English for the express purpose that they might be read and understood by people with no knowledge of Latin. A third series of Homilies completed in 996 or 997 shared the title of the earlier work but was clearly conceived independently. The style was more elevated than before and the subject matter restricted to saints' lives in calendar order, a primitive form of sacred biography which foreshadowed the later development of the hagiographical genre. Original thought was not demanded by his audience and the cult of the local saint was not yet a constraining influence. Although Aelfric's instinct was to interpret rather than merely translate, his adaptation of his source material did not extend beyond abridgment or expansion of certain passages and the insertion of the occasional personal comment or topical reference. His individuality lay in his handling of the Anglo-Saxon language, to which he applied the simplicity and clarity of his Latin style, and in his use of mixed prose and verse forms, the latter based loosely on Old English alliterative verse, but quite distinctive in character. The scribe of exhibit 90, an eleventh-century manuscript of the third book of Homilies, saw fit to guide the reader by marking with dots the ends of the lines of verse [46]. The volume once belonged to Bury St Edmunds Abbey, according to a thirteenth-century inscription. The passage illustrated is part of the homily for 20th November, the feast of its patron saint, which a modern editor has described as one of the most careful of Aelfric's compositions.

The upheaval of the Norman Conquest was reflected in intellectual life as well as in monastic organization. Abbots of Norman origin appointed by William to the major English monasteries brought new cultural values and a learning based on intensive study and imitation of the Latin classics. Outstanding among these abbots, both for his administrative ability and his literary talent, was Godfrey, prior of the Old Minster, Winchester. In accordance with his unassuming nature, little is known about his monastic background and the circumstances of his coming to England. The Norman reorganization of Winchester had already begun when he took office there in 1082, and in the twenty-five years of his rule, his personal reputation for hospitality, piety and learning transferred itself to the monastery. William of Malmesbury spoke of him as being 'distinguished in these times for literature and religion' and an anonymous epitaph called him 'a great philosopher and a worthy monk'. His literary fame rests on the *Liber Prouerbiorum,* a collection of two hundred and thirty-eight epigrams and poems in elegiac verse. Exhibit 91 is a late twelfth-century copy, reliable in its text but incomplete. In content and verse form, his professed model was Martial, and the imitation was so successful that in the later Middle Ages, Godfrey's works were often attributed to the Roman epigrammatist.

Godfrey understood the genre and wrote a pleasing Latin, but his monastic background blunted the sharpness of his wit and inhibited the biting or risqué remark, resulting in a style that is bland. Like Martial, he addressed his observations to fictitious persons, using mostly Roman names but with a few contemporary ones, and some of his own invention. In a verse prologue, he explained that his method was to indicate the truth in mockery, and in this respect he can be compared with the satirist Juvenal whose maxim was 'ridentem dicere verum'. Godfrey, however, was prepared to laugh at himself as well as others, and this mitigated the effects of his criticism. His theme was not, like Juvenal's, 'all human life', but the life he knew within the monastery walls, coloured by extensive reading of the scriptures, the classics, and the commonplaces of contemporary philosophy. He preached a positive message, although it might be expressed in terms of converses, advocating friendship, humility, honesty, true values and aspirations, and consideration for others. His moralizing, didactic tone was that of a Christian Horace, rather than the witty thrust of a Martial or the wounding sting of a Juvenal or Petronius, but none of the classical authors with whom he was obviously familiar would have been ashamed to acknowledge him as a successor.

The outlook and accomplishments of an ordinary monk born and bred on this side of the English Channel were inevitably very different from those of the immigrant Norman abbot. Eadmer was born in Kent about 1060 and had his first experience of monastic life as a child oblate at Christ Church, Canterbury under the Anglo-Saxon régime, before Lanfranc's reforms were thrust upon him in adolescence. All his life he maintained an ambivalent attitude to the Conquest, acknowledging that the reforms it brought were salutary at that time, but insisting that the traditions of the Anglo-Saxon past and especially the golden age of Dunstan had to be championed against foreign interference.

Had he remained in the cloister at Canterbury, slightly reactionary and unsure of his cultural identity, Eadmer might never have made his name as a writer. Circumstances, however, combined to give him opportunities on which even William of Malmesbury was to look with envy. As a kind of personal assistant to Archbishop Anselm, he travelled extensively in England and abroad, visiting the royal court, Rome and Cluny, attending councils at Bari and Rome, and meeting the ecclesiastical and secular dignitaries of Europe. His genuine admiration for Anselm inspired him to become his biographer, and from an early date he assiduously noted his conversations and copied the archival documents to which his post as keeper of the chapel gave him access. Anselm, finding his intention incompatible with proper humility, ordered the destruction of the draft, but Eadmer wisely kept a copy and resumed his work after his subject's death in 1109. The result was the *Vita Anselmi* and *Historia Nouorum in Anglia* conceived as a single work in two parts, treating separately the private and public life of the archbishop in the manner of Anglo-Saxon biography. The *Vita Anselmi* was pure biography, an intimate and perceptive character study surpassing

47. Eadmer, Historia Nouorum, *beginning of book V.*

48. Malmesbury Abbey. Watercolour by J. Buckler.

even those of Bede.

The *Historia Nouorum* by the nature of its subject, was history on a larger scale than any of its precursors, including biography, local, ecclesiastical, and institutional history within the framework of the dispute between church and state. As a result of his experiences inside and outside the cloister, Eadmer saw the issues at stake with remarkable clarity, but he was prone to oversimplify or make unconsidered judgments. His achievement was dictated by the material available to him and he was for-

tunate to have chosen a great man for the subject of his biography. His interest in detail made him a vivid eyewitness, original in his observation and analysis of contemporary events, but less sure of himself when dealing with the past. He wrote a good classical Latin which William of Malmesbury described as 'sober and pleasant'. The *Historia Nouorum,* which covers events from 1066–1122 with a sketch of the pre-Conquest background, was written in four books between 1109 and 1115, and two further books were begun in 1119. It was in these last books that Eadmer's weakness was revealed, and this too can be attributed to his circumstances. Archbishop Ralph who succeeded Anselm could never be a hero, for he failed to champion the cause of Christ Church. Eadmer himself was obliged to decline the offer of the archbishopric of St Andrews in Scotland, because of the implications his appointment might have for the Canterbury–York controversy. He was out of sympathy with a new generation of monks at Canterbury, and since his retirement from public affairs, he was obliged to spend more time in the monastery, in a discipline to which he was not accustomed. His earlier bias in favour of England and the English church descended to futile championship of Christ Church alone. Criticism of Anselm and later of himself made him defensive, causing him to suppress and distort the truth. In place of the eyewitness accounts and carefully recorded conversations which enlivened his early narratives, he resorted to copying forged documents, of whose nature he must have been aware, even if he had no part in their fabrication. Only two manuscripts of the *Historia Nouorum* survive, testifying to a lack of interest among contemporaries who already considered it a thing of the past. One, at Corpus Christi College, Cambridge, is probably Eadmer's autograph; exhibit 86 [47] is a copy of about a hundred years later, from which some of the documents have been omitted.

If Eadmer was an exception among Benedictines, a monk shaped by his experience of the world but biased by his monastic loyalties, William of Malmesbury and Matthew Paris who developed the historiographical genre were men of a different stamp. The former was, in the best sense, an English product of the Norman renaissance. As D.H. Farmer says, 'At this time, only a Benedictine monastery could have produced a William of Malmesbury.' Under abbot Godfrey of Jumièges, Malmesbury [48] provided both contact with the new learning and strong links with the Anglo-Saxon past through its associations with Aldhelm, Athelstan, and Dunstan. It was not a centre of profound scholarship (William complained of monks who were ignorant of Latin and were not even fluent in the vernacular), and it had no tradition of historical writing, but William's talents were not to be inhibited by lack of precedents. He must have found all the inspiration he needed in the library which he had helped to organize, as a precocious child of nine or ten, according to his own chronology. Soon after the age of thirty-two, he had produced two major historical works, the *Gesta Regum Anglorum* and the *Gesta Pontificum Anglorum.* History was not a by-product of his experiences, but a vocation. It is said that he twice refused the abbacy of Malmesbury, and he revised his work continuously until his death about 1143, tempering in his old age the harsher judgments of his youth. He wrote as a Benedictine for his fellows, knowing that within the cloister at least, his work was destined to survive. The existence of about twenty medieval manuscript copies of the *Gesta Pontificum* vindicates his confidence. His autograph text (exhibit 87) reveals his

49. William of Malmesbury, Gesta Pontificum.

method of working. The notebook in which it was written was of a size suitable for carrying with him as he travelled round the country in search of material. Erasures, interlineations, changes in word order indicated by superscript letters, changes in ink, and sentences inserted at the foot of the page, some with references to events much later than 1125 when the first draft was finished, bear witness to the constant process of revision [49]. The *Gesta Pontificum* was originally intended to be an appendix to the

50. *Matthew Paris, map of England and part of Scotland.*

Gesta Regum but it grew into a separate work, the ecclesiastical counterpart to the secular history. This division of subject matter was not new; William's originality lay in his arrangement of material on a geographical basis, starting in Book 1 with Canterbury and Rochester and concluding in Book 5 with Malmesbury. Denied Eadmer's contact with major events, he compensated with an antiquarian's zeal for research, noting details of topography and architecture as he saw them, and interweaving anecdotes which he heard or read with little exercise of critical judgment. In describing contemporary events, he lacked perspective and could be over-imaginative. His assessments of the past are generally sounder. His work was entertaining and instructive ('history teaches by example', as he said in the preface to the *Gesta Regum*) and in making the proviso that he could not vouch for the truth of all he wrote, William had the wisdom to admit the limitations of his own experience.

The cultural traditions of St Albans, where he took the habit in 1217, were fostered in the work of Matthew Paris. The foremost abbey in the country, it stood literally and metaphorically at the crossroads of ecclesiastical and secular England. Matthew with his lively mind, varied interests, and journalist's eye for drama, absorbed all that happened there and took advantage of his contact with the people who passed through. He was also able to travel more widely in England than the average monk, perhaps on account of some special but unrecorded position which he held in the monastery, although he apparently only went abroad on one occasion. In the view of Antonia Gransden, his intellectual motivation was his Benedictinism. A chronical of St Albans had already been begun by Roger of Wendover. Matthew succeeded him as official historian, but with a completely different attitude to history. Research and book-learning were not his methods. He drew instead on a store of personal knowledge in an astounding variety of fields: domestic, ecclesiastical, local and political history, as well as art, architecture, heraldry, and science. His background was the whole European scene, of which he showed an appreciation unique in his time, but despite such breadth of vision, he was not immune from personal bias, particularly against change and centralized authority.

Inevitably, his work took on encyclopaedic proportions, and Matthew was obliged to make separate compilations of additional material and epitomes to guide the reader. Revision became the obsession of his old age. The *Historia Anglorum* represented a reworking of the *Chronica Majora* in which Matthew attempted to confine himself to matters relevant to England between the Conquest and his own day. Exhibit 88 is his autograph manuscript with his own additions and corrections. The preliminary matter, which is not connected with the text, includes the well-known drawing of the Virgin and Child [**col. IV**], which illustrates the artistic side of Matthew's genius. An example of his mature style as seen in the poise and sensitivity of the facial expressions, it was probably executed between 1240 and 1250. It was a work of balanced contrasts: the statuesque Virgin and crouching monk, the thick and thin lines, the careful detail and the sketched impression, although heavy shading spoils the overall effect. In some respects, it looked back to the Transitional style which was already on the wane, but it also anticipated the revival of the Anglo-Saxon technique of line-drawing which was to become the hall-mark of the St Albans school founded by Matthew Paris. Cartography was another of his interests, as is shown in exhibit 85 [**50**]. The handwriting and the drawings, which foreshadow the use of conventional symbols, are certainly his own, but it is impossible to tell how far the compilation was original. Unlike most medieval maps, north is at the top, making it sympathetic to the modern eye. The map seems to be aligned along the route from Dover to Newcastle. St Albans is therefore prominent in the centre, although the south of England is distorted. Matthew was aware of his debt to his abbey, and in tacit recognition, he recorded the donation of four autograph manuscripts 'to God and St Albans'.

Benedictine monasteries attached great importance to record keeping and especially to their chronicles and annals which recorded their history from the date of foundation and the achievements of successive abbots. Most of the chroniclers were anonymous or virtually so, like John of Glastonbury, who flourished about 1400, of whom nothing is known except his name. The prologue to his history of Glastonbury is a clear explanation of the chronicle tradition, an account of the criteria by which one writer extended and adapted the work of previous generations. John saw his task as 'following in the footsteps of the monk William of Malmesbury . . . and brother Adam of Domerham'. He added many things which William had omitted from his *De Antiquitate Glastoniensis Ecclesiae* and rearranged the whole, as he considered, in better order. Adam of Domerham (d. after 1291), cellarer and sacristan of Glastonbury, continued William's work with the stated object of encouraging his readers to protect or increase the prosperity of the church. In John's opinion, Adam was too much inclined to prolixity. He shortened this section in his own history and extended it beyond Adam's time to about 1400. In a commonplace apology, he spoke of his own rude style and uncouth speech, but insisted that truth was his chief concern. The truth of his own sources, saints' lives and 'ancient books', apparently went unquestioned, although he mentioned contradictions which he found and the difficulty of collating different authorities. He not only inserted everything he could find about the mythical founding of Glastonbury by Joseph of Arimathea, and about the connection with King Arthur, he even produced a family tree to link the two characters. William, on the other hand, had been sceptical about Arthur. Exhibit 89, a curious manuscript bound along the short sides of the leaves, is an incomplete version of the chronicle which ends in 1334 with the account of prior John of Breynton. Another manuscript in the Bodleian Library contains not only the rest of John's composition but a continuation from 1400 to 1493 by another Glastonbury monk, perhaps Thomas Wason.

The monastic orders did not lack critics in the Middle Ages. Satirists such as Walter Map and Gerald of Wales are well-known for their strictures of monks of all colours, but it is unusual to find a monk satirizing monasticism from within. The freedom of thought and expression prevailing in the Benedictine milieu is exemplified in the work of Nigel, a monk of Christ Church, Canterbury, sometimes surnamed Wireker or Longchamps. He joined the community before 1170, for he claimed personal acquaintance with Thomas Becket. In connection with the dispute between Archbishop Baldwin and the monks, he was given the responsibility of a mission to Rome. His activities reflected a particular concern with loss of monastic privileges and increasing secularization in some houses, but his satire, far from being the product of a personal grievance, ranged over the whole field of commonplace errors and vices, both secular and ecclesiastical. The *Speculum Stultorum*, which was written sometime before 1180, followed the tradition of the animal fable or beast epic. The protagonist was an ass who travelled across Europe in search of a longer tail, attempting on the way to acquire a university education and found a new religious order, before being ignominiously reclaimed by his master and put to his proper use as a beast of burden. The second part of the poem, only loosely connected with the first, was really a sermon on ingratitude, resulting from the experience of the ass's master in rescuing a rich man and three wild animals from a pit. This was satire in the true classical sense of a mixture, combining within the framework of one elegiac poem a diversity of characters and situations, interspersed with independent fables, exempla, sermons and debates, and enlivened with rhetorical topics, proverbs, allusions, puns and parodies. The ass, called Burnellus or Brunellus in the poem but more familiar as Chaucer's Dan Burnel, was equated in the prologue with 'a monk or anyone in orders who, although meant like the ass to bear the burdens of the Lord, is not content with the natural order of things . . . but desires the office of prior or abbot . . . which, if obtained, he will wave about proudly like a tail'.

Nigel's satire was light-hearted; he preferred burlesque to invective, and while he could be crude, he was never offensive. Criticism could still be effective if tinged with Christian charity. In one section of the poem, Burnellus reviewed the existing religious orders as he deliberated which he should join, and finding them all unsatisfactory, he decided to found a new one of his own, incorporating from each the elements most congenial to himself. Nigel described his technique in this delicate subject in the prologue, saying that he made his accusations in a jocular fashion because a wound usually responds better to ointment than to caustic. The Benedictines were naturally spared his examination, but the Cluniacs, to whom they were most akin, were mocked for the generosity of their diet of eggs, beans and salt, supplemented by fats and meats on Fridays, the luxury of their fur-lined clothes, and their private possessions. Excessive strictness could be as reprehensible as laxity. The Cluniacs also incurred criticism for their habit of rising at midnight for the night office, and for their endless chants in which even the unskilled and the unfit were expected to join. Punishments for misbehaviour were too severe and the abbots too authoritarian. The Cistercians, in the character of Froumondus as well as in the special review, were accorded the harshest treatment, and the other orders fell between these extremes.

The *Speculum Stultorum* found a wide audience, as is attested by frequent quotation and imitation, and the fact that there are thirty-nine extant manuscripts from the fourteenth and fifteenth centuries. Exhibit 92 is a mid-fifteenth-century copy, in which the poem is prefaced by a letter to William Longchamp, bishop of Ely and later Chancellor, explaining the allegory, and the margins are adorned with engaging sketches of asses and monks.

Two hundred years later, the liberalization of monastic principles had progressed so far that John Lydgate, a professed Benedictine monk, was able to divide his time between the cloister and the world. There is controversy over how much of his time was spent within the walls of Bury, whose outstanding library must have furnished

51. *John Lydgate,* The glorious lyfe and passion of seint Albon . . ., *the martyrdom of St Alban (woodcut).*

his source material. Some authorities think his massive output of verse could only have been achieved by one who shut himself away in the cloister. Others argue from the evidence of his travels and contacts at court, his position equivalent to that of a poet laureate, and his financial status, that his links with the monastery cannot have been more than tenuous. Certainly as prior of Hatfield Broadoak in Essex from 1421–1434 he spent very little time in residence. Patronage was the key factor in Lydgate's success. He wrote to order, and orders came from court and nobility as well as from ecclesiastical dignitaries.

The Lives of St Alban and St Amphibal (exhibit 93) was written in 1439 at the request of John Whethamstede, abbot of St Albans, himself an author of note. Wishing to have an account of his abbey's patron saint, the 'protomartyr of England', he commissioned Lydgate to produce a similar 'double biography' to that of St Edmund and St Fremund which had been commissioned for Bury (exhibit 71). The work was duly completed and its author paid £3. 6s. 8d., according to the St Albans register. Meanwhile, Whethamstede resigned his office, relying on his successor to ensure that the finished book found its proper place at the shrine of the saint. However, when he entered his second period as abbot, he found it cast aside and neglected, still unbound. He immediately retrieved the loose sheets and had them bound in a fitting manner. Lydgate's merits as a poet are disputed and cannot be discussed here, but the Life of St Alban was not one of his best works, for it was marred by digressions and superfluous rhetoric. He claimed to have translated from French and Latin versions, but he conveyed the sense rather than the word and had no scruples about adding material of his own. As an epic legend written for a sophisticated audience, it owed very little to the popular saints' lives of religious or didactic purpose.

It is appropriate to conclude a chapter which began with manuscript production in Benedictine monasteries with a mention of printing, a commercial venture from the start in which monks could never hope to take a leading part. Only three English monasteries, Abingdon, St Albans and Tavistock, all Benedictine, were involved with printing at an early date, and only at Tavistock has it been proved that the work was done by monks. At St Albans, a professional secular printer, John Herford, was active between 1526 and 1538 under the patronage of the abbots Catton and Stevenage. Two examples of his work are exhibits 37, a breviary of c.1526, and exhibit 94, Lydgate's Lives of St Alban and St Amphibal of 1534 [51]. The manuscripts produced by the Benedictines are the relics of a past age, but printing continues to be a monastic art, if only a minor one, represented in its modern form by exhibit 47, a ritual printed by nuns of Stanbrook Abbey in 1963.

Rachel Stockdale

DISSOLUTION

N March 1540, virtually six hundred years after St Dunstan's refoundation of Glastonbury, the last remaining monasteries in England surrendered to King Henry VIII. The final Benedictine houses to go were Christ Church, Canterbury and St Andrew's, Rochester. Their fall marked the successful conclusion of a campaign to eradicate monasticism, set in motion by Cardinal Wolsey who, between 1525 and 1528 had found his first victims in fifteen of the smaller Benedictine foundations. Black monks were generally no better or worse than their brethren in other orders, but their monasteries were usually richer and their properties more desirable, as statistics from the *Valor Ecclesiasticus* prove. This nationwide survey of clerical incomes, compiled in 1534, showed some eighty-six Benedictine houses with net incomes under £200 a year, and some fifty-six with incomes above. The former came under the provisions of the Act for the Dissolution of the Lesser Monasteries in 1536 and were, with a few exceptions, automatically suppressed. Of the five wealthiest monasteries in Britain which reaped over £2,000 a year, four were Benedictine: Westminster Abbey, Glastonbury, Christ Church, Canterbury and St Albans. Sixteen other Benedictine houses, including the nunnery at Shaftesbury, recorded incomes at this time of between £1,000 and £2,000 a year.

Whilst it could form a basis for legislation, income alone could not provide any justification for suppression. Incriminating evidence was needed, and to this end Thomas Cromwell, the king's vice-regent in matters spiritual, sent out his representatives in 1535 to visit all monasteries and make reports. Some results of their labours are preserved in a British Library manuscript, Cotton MS. Cleopatra E. iv. Besides the formal visitation documents, the instructions, injunctions and certificates, there are the more revealing informal letters to Cromwell from his henchmen, asking for advice or reporting progress. Exhibit 104 is one such letter from John Ap Rice at Bury St Edmunds. Ap Rice, a lawyer by profession, had set out in August in the company of Thomas Legh, another equally notorious commissioner, on a visitation which took them through Wiltshire, Hampshire and the Thames Valley into East Anglia. Of necessity, their enquiries were conducted at speed, for there was much ground to be covered, but a surprising amount of detail was collected. The letter from Bury opened with an appraisal of the abbot. 'As for the abbot,' wrote Ap Rice, 'we found nothing suspect touching his living.' However, the commissioners considered that he spent too much time away from the monastery at his outlying granges, that he wasted money on gambling and on ambitious building projects, and that he neglected his duty of preaching in public, a common fault, it seems, among contemporary abbots. Complaints about his conduct as a landlord had been raised by disgruntled tenants who found their secure freehold tenures suddenly converted to copyhold. The abbot was clearly a traditionalist who had failed to move with the times, in that he continued to practise 'such superstitious ceremonies as have been used heretofore', and it was reported that women had been frequenting the monastery precincts. On questioning the monks, the commissioners encountered a conspiracy of silence, an attitude dictated by prudence and by no means unique to Bury.

In the absence of any serious accusation, a large part of the letter was concerned with relics. Cromwell was particularly concerned to locate and remove the objects of popular superstition which stood in the way of religious reform, and he had possibly given special instructions that they should be listed. Ap Rice described with a refreshing touch of humour the oddly assorted collection: the coals which toasted St Lawrence, the parings of St Edmund's nails, St Thomas Becket's penknife and boots, various skulls for curing headaches, enough pieces of the True Cross to make up a complete cross, and relics to produce rain and prevent weeds from growing in corn. In conclusion, statistics were mentioned: eight members of the community were under age, five adults 'of the best sort in the house' would leave if given the opportunity, fifty-nine monks were resident, and three were away studying at Oxford.

The commissioners' concern with relics finds an interesting sequel in another letter in the same volume. Even though Bury, the eighth house in the country in respect of its income, was immune from suppression at this time, it could not be allowed to continue as a place of pilgrimage. 'We have been at St Edmund's Bury', reported a new commission under John Williams, 'where we found a rich shrine which was very cumbrous to deface.' Despite the difficulty, the job was done thoroughly, and the memorial of St Edmund, king and martyr, was destroyed in the abbey to which he gave his name.

Athelney Abbey in Somerset has been chosen to illustrate the process of voluntary surrender because its decline is particularly well documented. With a net income of £210 a year, according to the *Valor Ecclesiasticus*, it just escaped suppression under the act of 1536, but it was already in serious financial difficulties. In April of that year, the abbot Robert Hamley wrote to Cromwell asking for help with the abbey's debts and hinting that he needed to borrow £400 or £500 to avoid bankruptcy. He appended to the letter a list of fifty-seven creditors to whom a total sum of £869. 12s. 7d. was owed. Debts of this size, more than four times the annual income, were unprecedented for a monastic house. The immediate outcome of the request is not known, but in November 1538, a year after the campaign against the remaining monasteries had been renewed, John Dycensen, rector of Holford, was deputed to discover the prospects of a voluntary surrender of Athelney. He sent a lively account

of his conversation with the abbot to Cromwell. A hint that the Lord Chancellor, Thomas Audley, was interested in making the house his own residence, together with promises of a bribe of a hundred marks for the abbot and proper provision for the monks, eventually persuaded Hamley to yield, although he demurred at the bribe, which he considered inadequate. The monks, more vociferous than those at Bury, expressed their willingness to surrender to the king.

52. *Deed of surrender of Athelney Abbey.*

The deed of surrender (exhibit 105, [**52**]) was dated 8th February 1539. In the terms of a conventional deed of gift or feoffment, the usual means of conveying freehold property, it transferred to the king, his heirs and assigns for ever, all rights of the monastery, however acquired. Emphasis was placed on the fact that the transaction was made 'after due consideration, freely and voluntarily'. A clause of warranty promised to uphold the king's title, and a special provision allowed him to dispose of the property at will, without interference from the former owners. Most deeds of surrender were, like this one, in Latin, but a few were in English. Nearly all were identical in wording, which suggests that they were copied out as required from a draft by a clerk who accompanied the commissioners. The names of the abbot of Athelney and six monks appear as witnesses in the left-hand margin, although it is a matter of controversy whether or not they were genuine signatures. The commissioner who took the surrender was John Tregonwell whose name is at the foot of the deed. The conventual seal of Athelney is attached to the document, a well preserved impression in red wax showing Christ between St Peter and St Paul in canopied niches.

Deeds of surrender were returned for safe-keeping to the Court of Augmentations, an instrument of central government set up in 1536 to administer the lands and properties of dissolved monasteries on behalf of the Crown. The need for revenue to meet the king's expenses and to pay the monks' pensions meant that the lands had to be sold or leased as soon as possible, and despite the wording of the surrenders, it was never intended that the king should become the permanent owner. Exhibit 107 is a contemporary copy of a grant recorded on one of the compotus rolls of the Court of Augmentations. By letters patent dated 4th March 1540, the site and lands, granges, rights and taxes of Ramsey Abbey, ennumerated in considerable detail, were conveyed to Richard Williams, alias Cromwell, a nephew of Thomas Cromwell. Richard had visited Ramsey as a commissioner in October 1538 when he reported that he found the abbot 'conformable to everything'. A favourable impression formed on that visit had perhaps persuaded him to stake his claim. The price was high: a down-payment of £4,963. 4s. 2d. and an annual rent of £29. 16s. to be paid into the Court of Augmentations for the king's use. The investment proved a good one, however, for it is recorded that the family made a flourishing business of selling stone from the abbey for building purposes. Other abbeys such as Whitby (exhibit 110, [53]) met a less dignified fate, being left to fall into ruin when no further use could be foun for them.

The value of Henwood priory in Warwickshire was considerably less than that of Ramsey Abbey, but the royal letters patent granting it to John Hygford (exhibit 111) were nonetheless impressive. The priory had been dissolved in 1536, when it had an income of £21 a year and only six nuns and a retired prioress were in residence. The new owner who acquired it on 26th February 1540 was apparently a local landowner, probably a relative of the last prioress, Alice Higford. Beneath an illuminated headline, which included a portrait of the king in the first initial, the document detailed the property, all of it in Warwickshire, and stipulated an initial payment of £207. 5s., followed by an annual rent of 23s. 1d. Two receipts attached to the left-hand margin from the Treasurers of Augmentations, Edward North and John Pope, recorded the two instalments of the down-payment. The receipts were in English but the document itself was in Latin. The Great Seal of England was appended on a green and white plaited cord.

Lands and buildings were not the only assets of the dissolved monasteries. Movable items of value were impounded by the commissioners and speedily conveyed to the king's treasury. More permanent fixtures were inventoried and left to await collection, or sold locally. Books were of special interest to King Henry VIII for augmenting his private library (see chapter 5). Exhibit 106 gives some insight into the royal selection procedure. It is a list of books, chiefly on the subjects of history or divinity, found in thirty-five monastic houses in north and east Lincolnshire just prior to their dissolution. The compiler was probably John Leland, the King's Antiquary, although the list is not in his handwriting. Clearly he was commissioned to record only certain kinds of books, for in some cases he noted in passing the presence of other works in manuscript not relevant in subject matter, or of printed books. Two houses could not be visited because of outbreaks of the plague. At another, the absence of the prior prevented a proper inspection. After the list had been made, it was apparently

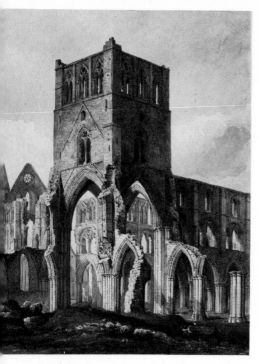

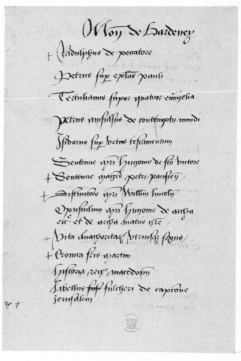

53. *Whitby: the ruins of the Abbey. Water-colour by J. C. Buckler.*

54. *List of manuscripts in Lincolnshire monasteries, by John Leland (?), books at Bardney.*

given to the king who marked with a cross in the margin some thirty-five items which he particularly desired. It is fairly certain that these crosses were made by Henry himself, because a note in the same ink on folio 2b is recognized as being his own hand. Folio 5b [54] shows the list for Bardney Abbey, one of the largest Benedictine houses in the area. Thirteen books were listed and five of them were marked with a cross. All five can be identified, by means of their contents and inscriptions connecting them with Bardney, with manuscript volumes now in the British Library. Four are in the Royal collection and must have fallen into the hands of the king soon after the list was made. They include two volumes of miscellaneous theological treatises (now Royal MSS. 7 A. iii and 10 A. vii), the Sententiae of Peter the Lombard (probably Royal MS. 9 B. ix) and the *Chronicle of Popes and Emperors* by Martinus Polonus (Royal MS. 13 A. vii). For some reason the fifth book, a Rule for Anchorites, was not acquired by the king, but found its way into the library of the book-collector Sir Robert Cotton. There it was severely damaged by fire, but enough remains, including part of the Bardney inscription, to identify it with the tenth book on Leyland's list. It is now in the British Library, bound with other items as Cotton MS. Vitellius E. vii. The survival of a few books whose history can be traced with certainty should not be allowed to obscure the fact that the majority of monastic books were destroyed at the Dissolution, some deliberately because their contents were considered offensive in the new religious climate, others by reuse as note-books and wrapping paper by people who were ignorant of their real value.

Attitudes to the threat of dissolution varied among the ordinary monks. Some were
only too glad to be released from their vows and to re-enter the world. Others clung
to the monastic life, transferring to other houses while the option remained open to
them. None was left completely destitute, as pensions based on the status of each
monk in his community were paid until alternative means of support could be found.
Pershore in Worcestershire was one of the last Benedictine abbeys to be closed, on
21st January 1540. One of its inmates, Richard Beerly, had foreseen the end some four
years previously and had turned circumstances to his own advantage by writing a
sycophantic letter to Thomas Cromwell, begging to be released from his vows
because he could not tolerate the laxity of the community. 'The religion which we do
observe and keep,' he wrote, 'is no rule of St Benedict, nor yet no commandment of
God, nor of no saint.' He complained of monks drinking and playing cards and dice

56. *Cromwell's Remembrances, directions for the trial and execution of the last abbots of Reading and Glastonbury.*

55. *Survey of the lands of Colchester Abbey, drawing symbolising the execution of the last abbot.*

until late in the evening and then appearing half way through matins 'drunk as mice'. In 1539, the abbot John Stonywell, under threat of indictment for treason on account of some unguarded statements about papal supremacy, expressed his willingness to surrender in return for pensions for himself and his monks 'according to their virtues'. A contemporary book of pensions from the Court of Augmentations, now in the Public Record Office, recorded awards to fourteen monks at Pershore ranging from the abbot at the top of the list to a certain Thomas Heathe at the bottom. Exhibit 108 is the deed by which the grant was made to the same Thomas Heathe. It was dated 12th February, just three weeks after the surrender, and it stated that he was to receive six pounds a year until he were promoted to an ecclesiastical benefice or benefices of that or greater value. The brown wax seal was that of the Court of Augmentations, the witness was the Chancellor, Sir Richard Rich. Four other monks at Pershore received pensions of similar value, the rest received more. Five pounds was considered the usual pension for a fully professed monk, so perhaps the status of a powerful abbot or his begging letter had moved the Court of Augmentations to generosity.

After the fall of the Cluniac priory of Lewes in 1537, the outcome of the renewed campaign against the monasteries was inevitable. With the passing of the Act for the Dissolution of the Greater Monasteries in 1539, it was clear that the king would succeed in closing the remaining houses and seizing their lands, if not with their cooperation, then by contrived legal actions against the abbots. Anyone who continued to resist was judged by contemporary opinion to be either a fool or a martyr. Five heads of houses did persevere in their resistance: three Benedictine abbots at Colchester, Reading and Glastonbury, one Cluniac prior at Lenton, and one Cistercian abbot at Woburn. The executions of the last two for alleged treason at the end of 1538 were mere preliminaries. It was the *cause célèbre* of the three Benedictine abbots, who died within a fortnight in November and December 1539, that forced the remaining monasteries into surrender and wound up the whole operation by March 1540.

Thomas Beche of Colchester, Hugh Cook of Reading, and Richard Whiting of Glastonbury had all shown exceptional promise in their early careers, which had led to appointments as heads of influential houses. All had enjoyed the king's favour, all had apparently subscribed to the Act of Supremacy, and all had paid the bribes necessary to maintain the privileged position of their houses in the early 1530s. Thomas Beche was the last to be executed, on 1st December. The indictment and report of his trial, now among the papers of the Court of the King's Bench at the Public Record Office, alleged that he had been heard to deny royal supremacy, to condemn the suppression of the monasteries, and to boast that he would never surrender voluntarily. A streak of indiscretion in his character, coupled with his staunchly conservative religious views, lends plausibility to the charge. Whilst he was awaiting his fate in the Tower of London, he attempted to retract the statements, but there could be no reprieve. Egerton MS. 2164 [55] shows at the head of a fragmentary abstract of Colchester Abbey lands, a drawing of a judge riding out of a town, whilst an abbot is being hanged in the background.

In chillingly decisive terms, Cromwell's famous 'Remembrance' (item 109, [56]) sealed the fates of Hugh Cook and Richard Whiting: 'Item the abbot of Reading to be sent down to be tried and executed at Reading with his accomplices'. 'Item the abbot of Glastonbury to be tried at Glastonbury and also executed there with his accomplices'. On the reverse of the page, he named the witnesses who were to give evidence, with a note: 'Item to see that the evidence be well sorted and the indictments well drawn against the said abbots and their accomplices.' Hugh Cook's indictment is still extant in the Public Record Office. The accusation was one of asserting and maintaining papal supremacy, which carried the penalty of death for treason. The 'accomplices' were John Eynon, priest of St Giles, Reading, and John Rugg, a retired prebendary from Chichester living at Reading. Even if the charge was justified, it did not tell the whole truth. Already in September of the previous year, the commissioner John London had hinted at the imminent surrender of Reading Abbey, and it appears from the correspondence that the abbot had actually acquiesced. His failure to cooperate at the last moment must have caused embarrassment in high places. As a mitred abbot, Hugh had a right to a hearing before Parliament, but Cromwell's Remembrance made no allowance for this, and formalities were clearly waived to ensure a speedy conclusion to the proceedings.

Richard Whiting of Glastonbury was the most tragic figure of the three great abbots. Appointed by Wolsey some fifteen years previously, he had run his house in exemplary fashion, the only complaint of his conduct being raised on one occasion by some monks who found him too strict. In September 1539 he was a sick man approaching seventy-five, and Glastonbury was the only monastery left in Somerset. Pollard, Moyle, and Layton arrived on a visit of inspection. They reported to Cromwell (in a letter now in the Bodleian Library, Oxford) that they had found in the abbot's study a book against the royal divorce, some copies of papal documents, and a printed biography of Thomas Becket, but not the incriminating letters, which by implication they had hoped to discover. Almost as an afterthought, they spoke of concealed valuables from the abbey having come to light, and their suspicion that the abbot had been involved in their removal. Meanwhile, having examined the abbot, they claimed that his answers to their questions revealed his 'cankered and traiterous heart and mind against the king's majesty and his succession'. This was sufficient to secure Whiting's arrest and imprisonment in the Tower. Trial at Wells followed on 14th November. There are no formal records extant, but a letter from Lord John Russell to Cromwell mentioned that the charge was 'the robbing of Glastonbury church'. Of the two monks tried at the same time, John Thorne and Roger James, the former had been abbey treasurer. Russell's letter and another from Richard Pollard enable the manner of Whiting's death to be reconstructed. The day after the trial at Wells, he was tied to a hurdle and dragged publicly through the streets of Glastonbury to Tor Hill. There he was hanged, begging as he died for God's mercy and the king's forgiveness, but refusing to give evidence against his fellow monks. His body was taken from the gallows and divided into four for distribution throughout the diocese, one quarter going to Wells, one to Bath, one to Ilchester, and one to Bridgwater. His severed head was fixed upon the abbey gate at Glastonbury, a warning to any who, in the name of religious belief, might dare to make a stand against the royal will.

REBIRTH

HE desire for the monastic life did not wholly perish among English men and women after the dissolution of the monasteries. The short-lived restoration of catholicism under Mary Tudor included on the queen's personal initiative a revival of the ancient royal abbey of Westminster with a community made up of survivors from several of the old monasteries. Within two years, however, following on the accession of Queen Elizabeth I, the house was again dissolved. But among the young men clothed there as novices was one Sigebert Buckley, who spent the rest of his long life in and out of gaols until in 1603 he was found by a new generation of English monks, to whom he was able to transmit a living continuity with the medieval Benedictine past. The motto of St Benedict's own abbey of Monte Cassino, 'succisa virescit' ('the felled tree flourishes again'), can fittingly be applied to this new generation of monks.

At first, individual men and women who felt the call entered monasteries abroad. For example, in 1580 Dame Joanna Berkeley, the daughter of an ancient Gloucestershire family, became a Benedictine nun at Rheims, and in 1597 was invited to become abbess of a new house at Brussels which was the first Benedictine foundation for English catholic exiles since the dissolution of the monasteries.

In a similar way, there were English men who joined Benedictine monasteries in Italy and Spain, many of them with a strong urge to return to their native country to work for the survival and propagation of the old faith.

To further their joint aim of living a Benedictine life while pursuing missionary activity, groups came together and founded English monasteries for men at Douai, in the Spanish Netherlands (1607), Dieulouard in Lorraine (1608), and in Paris (1615). A formal link between these houses was established by the reconstituting of the English congregation of black monks of St Benedict in 1619. In 1625 the English Benedictine Congregation was responsible for the foundation of a house of nuns at Cambrai in northern France (now at Stanbrook Abbey).

All this activity did not take place without arousing hostility, both among conflicting interests within the Benedictine order and also on the part of religious

57. *Bull 'Plantata' of Pope Urban VIII, first page and bulla.*

organizations outside. To put an end to this strife Pope Urban VIII in 1633 issued a bull [**57**], named from its opening word *Plantata,* which is regarded as the foundation charter of the English Benedictine Congregation as it is today. The original document is displayed as exhibit 125. This bull set up the constitution of the English Benedictine Congregation, or refounded it so far as that might be necessary. Besides granting many other rights and privileges, it confirmed the principle that the monks could perform pastoral work in England, even though many would not regard this as a suitable occupation for monks.

The bull also took into account the special status which Benedictines had enjoyed in the medieval church, by an institution which was virtually unique to England. The chapters of nine cathedrals were made up of monastic communities. In those chapters the monks had elected their own cathedral prior, who was the equivalent of the dean in a secular cathedral. The pope, therefore, decreed that until England should return to the catholic faith, the Benedictines were to continue to nominate cathedral priors to maintain their ancient claim. Although the English Benedictine Congregation no longer lays claim to these churches, the titles of cathedral priories such as Canterbury, Winchester, Durham, Ely, and Bath are still in use, being bestowed on senior members of the Congregation as marks of honour.

THE TRADITION OF LEARNING

This appeal to history was characteristic of the Congregation from its earliest years and soon began to manifest itself in several important books compiled by the monks, who sought to justify their presence in the English mission field by citing the examples of St Augustine of Canterbury and of the early Anglo-Saxon missionaries. Thus, Dom Augustine Baker, who had formerly practised as a lawyer, transcribed an immense quantity of medieval records as the basis for the *Apostolatus Benedictinorum in Anglia,* published at Douai in 1626, one of the earliest historical works of an Englishman to cite original documents *in extenso.* Learned historical studies continued to be a tradition within the reborn English Congregation, as it had been in the Middle Ages, and the order found new chroniclers, such as Dom Bennet Weldon in the eighteenth century, Dom Athanasius Allanson in the nineteenth century, and Cardinal Aidan Gasquet in our own age. Best known of all monastic historians in England is Dom David Knowles, whose four-volume survey of the monastic and religious orders in England has established itself as a classic (exhibit 114).

It was of the greatest assistance to Augustine Baker in his historical researches that he was at home in that circle of eminent historians and scholars which centred on Sir Robert Cotton, the antiquary whose magnificent collection, rich in medieval manuscripts rescued after the dissolution of the monasteries, was eventually to become the nucleus for the present British Library. The friendship between the two men is attested by an original autograph letter, still preserved among the Cottonian manuscripts and shown here as exhibit 112. In this letter, addressed to Cotton in 1629 from Cambrai, Baker, as spiritual adviser to the new English foundation there, writes on behalf of the nuns who were short of suitable reading matter, to ask the great collector 'to bestowe on them such bookes as you please, either manuscript or printed, being in English, conteining contemplation Saints' lives or other devotions.'

SPIRITUAL WRITINGS

This request itself makes plain how deeply and deliberately from its start the spiritual tradition inaugurated by Baker, and continued by succeeding generations of English monks and nuns, drew upon the rich treasure store of the English medieval mystics. One highly important example of the key role they sometimes played in preserving and transmitting England's mystical heritage concerns the masterpiece of the fourteenth-century anchoress, Juliana of Norwich. It is a fact that, apart from a few extracts in one late medieval manuscript, all surviving witnesses to the longer and fuller text of her *Revelations of Divine Love* derive from seventeenth-century English Benedictine sources. In other words, her matchless contribution to christian mysticism is fully known to us today only because her writings were copied and studied by Augustine Baker and his followers. One of these followers, the editor who in 1670

58. Augustine Baker, Sancta Sophia, *engraving of the author.*

first put into print the text of the *Revelations* and so gave it a wide European readership, was Dom Serenus Cressy, who had been a prominent Laudian churchman before he converted to catholicism and in 1648 joined the English Benedictines at Douai. Cressy probably never met Baker (who died in 1641) in person; his first encounter with a live Benedictine was doubtless with Dom Cuthbert Fursdon, Baker's young disciple who made the first post-Reformation English translation of the Rule of St Benedict and was living as chaplain to Lady Elizabeth Cary, the catholic mother of Cressy's patron Lord Falkland, at the latter's house at Burford. All four of Lord Falkland's sisters became nuns at Cambrai, and their home at Burford today shelters a community of anglican Benedictine nuns.

It was Cressy who compiled, from the many manuscript treatises which the master had left in the hands of his disciples, the two-volume digest of Augustine Baker's spiritual teaching known as *Sancta Sophia or Directions for the prayer of contemplation* (exhibit 113). Although Baker had often been a controversial figure within the order during his lifetime, Cressy's publication of his teaching in 1657 had the full authority of the president of the Congregation and was printed at the expense of Cressy's monastery of St Gregory at Douai. Prefixed to the work is an attractive engraved portrait of the author done from life [58], and opposite it a commendatory poem by a fellow-monk which happily sums up the book's central doctrine: 'To Pray is not to talke, or thinke, but love'.

From that time on, among his fellow Benedictines this classic of the spiritual life has exerted the widest and most profound influence, greater than that of any other work written in England after the Middle Ages. The monks and nuns have preserved this tradition both in their personal lives and in their writings. The doctrine and practice of prayer learnt from Augustine Baker by one of his earliest disciples, Dame Gertrude More, a great-great-grand daughter of St Thomas More and one of the founders of Cambrai, who died in 1633 aged only twenty-six, continues to be reflected centuries later in writers such as Bishop Hedley (d. 1915) and Abbot Chapman (d. 1933) and by living writers such as Dom Hubert van Zeller and Cardinal Hume, whose *Searching for God* reprints discourses given by him as abbot to his monks (exhibit 116).

THE RETURN TO ENGLAND

The pattern of English Benedictine foundations across the Channel had reached its fullest extent before the end of the seventeenth century with a dozen different communities. In these houses successive generations of monks and nuns led their relatively uneventful lives of prayer and work until the French Revolution drove these communities back into an England now prepared at least to give them refuge. It took fully twenty years for the scattered remnants to come together again and to find permanent homes. The task of restoring full community life and rebuilding cloister, church, and school occupied the first half of the nineteenth century. Then in 1856 the arrival at Ramsgate of English monks from the Cassinese Congregation in Italy started a new era of foundations. The new foundations have had three main sources. Monks and nuns of other congregations, notably from France and Germany, added honoured names to the roll-call of Benedictine foundations, which have taken their rightful place in the English scene. About the same time, within the Church of England, a movement to reintroduce the religious life led to the start of several communities of men and women, who live today under the rule of St Benedict. Finally, the English Congregation brought into existence two new monasteries. The process of further foundations from all these sources has continued to the present day with daughter houses both inside Britain and beyond the seas in North and South America and in India.

THE MISSION

The English Benedictine Congregation has always been 'missionary' in the sense that from its very origins a major work was seen to be the pastoral care of catholics in England and work for the restoration of the old faith. During the whole of the seventeenth century, the life of a missioner in England was always at risk; a number of the Benedictines died in prison or after ill-treatment, and nine monks of the Congregation, eight priests and one lay brother, were publicly executed for their faith and are venerated by the church as martyrs. Three among these were canonized in 1970. It was the custom, and still is, to send a printed notice of the death of any member of the Congregation to the brethren to ask for prayers for the deceased, but in the mortuary bill (exhibit 122) announcing the death of St Ambrose Barlow, a monk from Douai who was executed at Lancaster in 1641 after twenty-four years of apostolic ministry in his own native Lancashire, the president of the English Benedictines requests not prayers for his soul but offerings of thanks for his witness. A further proof of the honour rendered to these martyrs can be seen in the existence of small contemporary engraved portraits of them with inscriptions giving details of the day and manner of their death. These were put into circulation to encourage catholics to honour these martyrs and to celebrate their 'feast day'. Two such pictures here exhibited are those of Ambrose Barlow (exhibit 123) and of the Welshman, Blessed Philip Powel (exhibit 124), executed in 1646 at Tyburn in London after working in Somerset [59]. Apart from the conventional martyr attributes of rope and knife these portraits bear every mark of being authentic likenesses.

Not all missionary work in England involved the monks in these extreme hazards: for the most part the monks on the mission lived secluded lives, but during the three hundred and seventy-five years of its existence the English Benedictine Congregation has provided centres for saying mass at nearly four hundred different places in England and Wales. To this day there are still about fifty parishes served by the Benedictines in England, quite apart from the area surrounding each monastery. About eighty monk priests are now serving on these parishes. In addition to these missionary priests the English Congregation has provided a long line of bishops and vicars apostolic concerned with the pastoral care of the catholic flock. Since the restoration of the catholic hierarchy in England and Wales in 1850, three Benedictines have been the first bishops in their sees. Bishop Ullathorne was one of the outstanding ecclesiastics of the nineteenth century, who early in his priestly career worked in Australia as the first vicar general there before returning to England to take up his position as bishop of Birmingham. The present Cardinal Archbishop of

The R^d. Father Philip Powel, alias
Morgan, of y^e Order of S^t. Benedict
executed at Tyburn, June 30th.1646
in the 52th year of his Age.

Westminster, Basil Hume, was previously abbot of Ampleforth, and one of his auxiliaries, Christopher Butler, was abbot of Downside.

Outside England the most notable missionary activity was in Australia, whither the Benedictine Bede Polding was sent in 1835 to be the first vicar apostolic of Van Diemen's Land, and so to be the first bishop in Australia, and finally archbishop of Sydney with ten suffragans. In the forty-two years of his activity in Australia he is said to have travelled more than almost any other missionary in the catholic church, apart from St Francis Xavier. Exhibit 121 is an example from his voluminous correspondence. Written to his fellow-monk, Bishop Thomas Brown, it describes how in the previous month he had gone far beyond the limits of the colony and ridden upwards of nine hundred miles, having previously gone to Maitland, eighty miles to the north, and to save time 'submitted to the horrors of steam navigation'. He further describes his harassment at the hands of an anti-catholic judge in Sydney, and the progress of his seminary for training young priests for the Australian church.

Before his death Polding had founded houses for both monks and nuns in Australia, and also a new order of nuns — the Good Samaritans — which continues to flourish with well over a thousand present members spread throughout Australia and the islands of the Pacific. Several other English Benedictines worked with him in Australia, notably Charles Davies, first bishop of Maitland, and Bede Vaughan, who succeeded him as archbishop of Sydney.

The other important missionary venture has been to Peru, where three monks went out from Worth Abbey in 1969 to the very backward area of the Apurimac Valley. They have now moved to the poor slums of Lima, and have built a small monastery there to look after the pastoral needs of the destitute locality. One monk remains in the Apurimac Valley continuing the pastoral work there.

There was during most of the nineteenth century a succession of bishops from the English Benedictine Congregation in charge of the predominantly French island of Mauritius in the Indian Ocean, and Dom Ansgar Nelson was for many years a bishop in Sweden.

EDUCATION

Many in England today would associate the Benedictine monks with their great schools. It is true that at the present time the education of boys employs a great deal of the manpower, particularly among the houses of the English Benedictine Congregation, but it was not always so on this scale, even though it has always gone on.

Teaching of an academic sort is nearly always being carried on in a monastery because of the need to train the young monks, and when catholic education was prohibited in England, there was an obvious need to educate boys, even if they were not intending to follow a monastic vocation. But of the English monasteries in France in the seventeenth and eighteenth centuries only St Gregory's at Douai was providing an education for the sons of English catholics, and it was no accident that the founding fathers chose the university town which was also a centre for English catholic exiles and the home of Cardinal Allen's seminary for English secular priests.

◀ 59. *Engraving of the Blessed Philip Powel.*

The monks who were educating their own novices also took their place in the university halls, and there has been a long line of monks from the English Benedictine Congregation who have lectured and held professorial chairs in the universities of France and England, such as Dom Rudesind Barlow at Douai, Bishop Gabriel Gifford at Rheims, and recently Dom David Knowles at Cambridge.

After the expulsion of the monks at the Revolution, St Gregory's kept the continuity of its school, first at Acton Burnell, and then at Downside. St Laurence's which had not had a school at Dieulouard, started this form of education at Ampleforth in 1814. St Edmund's had no school in Paris, but after the revolutionary wars they returned to France and took over the former buildings of St Gregory's at Douai, and there kept a school until in 1903 they were again expelled from France as a result of the Laws of Association. They also have maintained their continuity by their present school in Berkshire, and have marked this by retaining the name of Douai.

The character of all these schools varied little from the seventeenth century to the end of the nineteenth. They were comparatively small, on occasion enrolling less than twenty boys, never more than a hundred, and the education offered laid great emphasis on religion and languages, especially the classics. The prospectus for Downside, produced in the 1850s (exhibit 127, [**60**]) is typical of the period.

In the twentieth century with the increasing demand for catholics to take their full place in public life and to go to the universities, the Benedictine schools began to make radical changes in their size and form. They now modelled themselves more closely on the lines of the traditional English public schools. Marked emphasis is still laid on the spiritual and religious formation of the boys, but the secular learning now covers a much broader field, the numbers are much larger and the buildings and facilities far more impressive. The brochure of Douai Abbey and School (exhibit 126) shows the complex plan and lay-out of a contemporary English Benedictine establishment.

Besides those schools already mentioned, there are now schools, ranging in number from three hundred to seven hundred and fifty boys, run by monks at Ramsgate, Belmont, Fort Augustus, Buckfast, Ealing, and Worth in Britain and by monks of the English Benedictine Congregation at Portsmouth, Washington, and St Louis in the USA.

Many of the communities of nuns maintained schools for English girls on the Continent, and during the nineteenth century in England, but they were very small, and now all have ceased to exist except for those at Dumfries, Andover, and Fernham.

In addition to these schools, Ampleforth maintains an official 'Private Hall' at Oxford, Downside a residential house at Cambridge; Ealing provides a series of lectures in conjunction with London University and the Westminster Adult Religious Education Centre; Washington has strong links with the Catholic University of America nearby. Worth has for several years promoted a series of Conferences for adult listeners which have attracted large audiences from all over south-east England. In addition to the usual school magazines, many of the communities produce

60. Prospectus of Downside School, Downside Abbey, Bath.

COLLEGE OF ST GREGORY THE GREAT, DOWNSIDE, NEAR BATH.

St. Gregory's College, Downside, near Bath.

In order to combine the advantages usually sought from Education at public schools with a greater attention than can generally be bestowed in them upon the character, conduct, progress, and comfort of each student, only a limited number of Pupils is admitted into this Establishment.

As it is of the utmost importance to youth, especially in these times, that they be well grounded in their Religion, the first and greatest care is, that its doctrines and duties be assiduously expounded and inculcated.

The usual course of Education comprises the English, French, Italian, Latin, and Greek Languages; History, Geography, Mathematics, Chemistry, Logic, Natural and Moral Philosophy, and Metaphysics; and as the College has been empowered by Royal Charter to present Candidates for Degrees at the London University, the studies are so directed as to meet the Examinations there required.

TERMS: FIFTY GUINEAS PER ANNUM.

For Students in Philosophy, (commencing with the Matriculation Year), SIXTY GUINEAS.

Private Rooms, (for the elder Students), TEN GUINEAS extra.

TO BE PAID HALF-YEARLY IN ADVANCE.

Clothing, Medicine, and Postage are additional items; also, Music, Dancing, and Drawing.

It is expected that each Student be provided with a Knife, and a Silver Fork and Spoon.

The Vacation is confined to Seven Weeks at Midsummer. Parents are required not to detain their children beyond its expiration, as the places of those who do not return punctually will be considered vacant, and will be filled up by new applicants. They are also requested not to ask their absence from the College at any other season.

Further particulars may be obtained from the Very Rev. J. N. Sweeney, *Prior*.

periodicals and the *Downside Review*, the *Ampleforth Journal*, the *Douai Magazine*, and *Laudate* (from Nashdom) (exhibits 117, 118, 119 and 120) all have had a wide reputation as organs of theological and historical learning.

LITURGICAL AND ARTISTIC WORK

The 'opus dei' or work of god, is still, as it has been for fifteen hundred years, the prime concern of the Benedictines, although in nearly every case the office is now performed in English, and the structure is simpler than that laid down by St Benedict in his rule.

But Benedictines continue the tradition of enshrining this work of god in the most splendid setting, architecturally, musically, ceremonially, and artistically. This preoccupation is marked by the fine chasuble woven and made up by the nuns of Stanbrook (exhibit 34) and by the abbot's mitre from Prinknash (exhibit 31). The magnificent *Rituale Abbatum* (exhibit 47) is an excellent example of the printing and binding done by the Stanbrook Abbey Press, and the set of altar vessels shows the standard of work produced by the pottery at Prinknash (exhibit 128).

Monks and nuns have also been leaders not only in liturgical research, of which *The Shape of the Liturgy* by Dom Gregory Dix (exhibit 115) is a good example, but also in the study, composition and performance of church music, where outstanding contributions have been, or are still being made by, for example, Dame Laurentia McLachlan, Dom Lawrence Bévenot, Dom Gregory Murray, Dom Anselm Hughes, Dame Felicitas Corrigan, and Dame Anne Field.

The backboards to many of the cases in the exhibition give examples of monastic architecture during the past thousand years, and the tradition continues both in the revived gothic of Buckfast, rebuilt on its ancient site, and also in the striking new churches, for example, at Worth abbey in Sussex and St Louis priory in the United States.

Besides monastic buildings properly so called, monks and nuns have also, as parish priests, teachers, landlords, and farmers, been responsible for the erection of further churches, schools, halls, and granges, in many parts of the country, in various architectural styles, to answer a very wide range of needs.

In addition to these obvious and massive works the monks and nuns still contribute to the artistic heritage of their countries by such works as the stained glass made at Buckfast and Pluscarden. Many, if not most of the communities have members who produce paintings, drawings, carvings, engravings, needlework, and calligraphy, of a very high quality.

SUGGESTIONS FOR FURTHER READING

C. Butler, *Benedictine Monachism*, 1924.

I.B. Cowan and D.E. Eason, *Medieval Religious Houses: Scotland*, 1976.

D. Knowles, *The Monastic Order in England*, Cambridge, 1963.

D. Knowles, *The Religious Orders in England*, three volumes, Cambridge, 1948–1959.

D. Knowles, *The Monastic Constitutions of Lanfranc*, 1951.

D. Knowles and R.N. Hadcock, *Medieval Religious Houses: England and Wales*, 1971.

J. McCann, *The Rule of Saint Benedict in Latin and English*, 1952.

R.W. Southern, *Saint Anselm and his Biographer: A Study of Monastic Life and Thought 1059–c.1130*, Cambridge, 1963.

T. Symons, *The Monastic Agreement of the Monks and Nuns of the English Nation*, 1953.

R. Vaughan, *Matthew Paris*, Cambridge, 1958.

G.W.O. Woodward, *The Dissolution of the Monasteries*, 1966.

LIST OF EXHIBITS

1. Dialogues of St Gregory the Great. Royal MS. 6 B. ii. Latin, thirteenth century. Vellum, 112 folios. 31cm × 21cm. One historiated initial. Fourteenth-century ex-libris of Rochester Cathedral priory, 'Liber de claustro Roffensi per H. cantorem'. For other Rochester books see chapter 5 and exhibits 96–103.

2. Rule of St Benedict. Harley MS. 5431. Latin, c.1000, thirteenth and fourteenth centuries. Vellum, 122 folios. 23cm × 9cm. Composite volume. The rule belongs to the part executed c.1000, apparently at St Augustine's Abbey, Canterbury. This part is illuminated with decorated initials and motifs of similar design. Press-mark of St Augustine's, ex-libris, 'Et est liber Sancti Augustini Cant.', and fourteenth-century list of contents, the same as at present.

3. Psalter, with miniature of St Benedict and monks. Arundel MS. 155. Latin and Anglo-Saxon, after 1012, with twelfth-century additions. Vellum, iv + 193 folios. 29.2cm × 21cm. The original part was written at, and for, Christ Church Cathedral priory, Canterbury, by the Christ Church monk Eadvius Basan. It has illumination, probably by him, including two drawings, decorated and historiated initials, with associated borders, and the miniature of St Benedict. Ex-libris of the Christ Church monks, William Ingram and John Waltham, to the second of whom it was given by William Hadley, sub-prior of Christ Church.

4. Passional, including the Translation of St Benedict (11th July). Arundel MS. 169. Latin, twelfth century. Vellum, i + 103 folios. 34cm × 22.5cm. Contains feasts from the 'Passio sancti petri apostoli' (29th June) to St Alexius Confessor (17th July).

5. Miniature of St Dunstan (removed from exhibit 6). Royal MS. 10 A. xiii, f. 2b.

6. Smaragdus, *Commentary on the Rule of St Benedict*. Royal MS. 10 A. xiii. Latin, late twelfth century. Vellum, 156 folios. 24.5cm × 17.5cm. Written and illuminated apparently at Christ Church Cathedral priory, Canterbury. One miniature (exhibit 5). Fourteenth-century ex-libris of Christ Church. Subsequently belonged to Thomas Cranmer, archbishop of Canterbury.

7. Regularis Concordia. Cotton MS. Tiberius A. iii. Latin and Anglo-Saxon, second half of eleventh century. Vellum, 179 folios. 28.8cm × 23cm. Composite volume. Written and illuminated probably at Christ Church Cathedral priory, Canterbury. Two miniatures.

8. Lanfranc, Monastic Constitutions. Cotton MS. Claudius C. vi. Latin, second quarter of twelfth century, thirteenth, and fourteenth centuries. Vellum, 205 folios. 32.5cm × 21cm. Composite volume. The Monastic Constitutions belong to the twelfth-century part and originally made up a volume with Royal MS. 7 E. vi, a martyrology of Christ Church Cathedral priory, Canterbury, where they and it were presumably executed.

9. Constitutions of Pope Benedict XII for the Benedictines, 1336. Cotton MS. Faustina A. vi. Latin, fourteenth and fifteenth centuries. Vellum, 170 folios. 24cm × 14.5cm. Composite volume.

10. Account of the First Meeting of the Provincial Chapter of the English Benedictines, 1338. Additional MS. 6162. Latin, fifteenth century. Paper and vellum,

48 folios. 22cm × 14.5cm. Composite volume. Executed possibly at Durham Cathedral priory.

11. Glastonbury Abbey from the west end of the nave. Watercolour. Additional MS. 17463, ff. 132b–133. 32cm × 39.8cm. From Additional MSS. 17456–17463, collections for the history of several of the counties of England, by the Rev. D.T. Powell, nineteenth century.

12. Glastonbury Abbey, the interior of the lady chapel. Watercolour, 1816. Additional MS. 17463, f. 134. 19.5cm × 22.6cm. From the same collections as exhibit 11.

13. Glastonbury Abbey, the exterior of the lady chapel. Watercolour. Additional MS 17463, f. 135. 18.5cm × 25cm. From the same collections as exhibits 11 and 12.

14. Canterbury, the remains of Christ Church Cathedral priory. Watercolour by J. Buckler, 1804. Additional MS. 32357, f. 73. 24.2cm × 34.3cm. From Additional MSS. 32353–32375, drawings and watercolours, with prints and engravings, collected by J.W. Jones, to illustrate E. Hasted's *History of Kent*, eighteenth and nineteenth centuries.

15. Canterbury, the baptistery and library at Christ Church Cathedral priory. Watercolour by J. Buckler, 1804. Additional MS. 32357, f. 43. 26cm × 34.3cm. From the same collections as exhibit 14.

16. Instruction of novices according to the practice of St Augustine's Abbey, Canterbury. Cotton MS. Faustina C. xii. Latin, *c.*1330. Vellum, 202 folios. 30.3cm × 19cm. The Instruction of novices forms an independent chapter, preceded by a fragment of a customary and followed by documents relating to two abbots, another complete customary and additional notes on monastic practice. Three of these other compilations also deal with the profession and discipline of novices. Written at St Augustine's. The monogram on the fly-leaf may be that of John Mankael, monk of the abbey, who donated several books to its library.

17. Pontifical, including the ceremony of monastic profession. Cotton MS. Claudius A. iii. Latin and Anglo-Saxon, second half of tenth century, second quarter of eleventh century, and first half of twelfth century. Vellum, 150 folios. 24cm × 15.5cm. Miniatures. Composite volume consisting of three fragmentary pontificals with other material. The profession ceremony is found in the second pontifical, which was written at Christ Church Cathedral priory, Canterbury, in the second quarter of the eleventh century.

18 and 19. The Prayer-book of Aelfwine. Cotton MSS. Titus D. xxvi and xxvii. Latin and Anglo-Saxon, *c.*1023–1035. Vellum, 2 vols, 80 and 93 folios. 13cm × 9.5cm. Offices of the Holy Cross and Trinity with calendar, tables, *etc.* Copied at Winchester, partly by Aelsine, a monk, for the use of Aelfwine, dean and from 1035 abbot of the New Minster. Three full-page tinted drawings.

20. The Liber Albus of Bury St Edmunds Abbey. Harley MS. 1005. Latin, thirteenth and fourteenth centuries. Vellum, 281 folios. 23cm × 14cm. A volume of miscellaneous records and memoranda compiled by the monks of Bury, including a customary of the abbey and the chronicle of Jocelin of Brakelond. Composite volume. Bound with Harley MS. 498, vellum and paper documents relating to Bury.

21. Battle Abbey. Watercolour by William Buckler. Additional MS. 37120, no. 6. 30.5cm × 42.5cm. From Additional MSS. 37120–37146, architectural, topographical, and other watercolours and drawings by John Buckler (d. 1851), his son John Chessell Buckler (d. 1894), his grandson Charles Alban Buckler (d. 1905), and other members of the Buckler family. Bequeathed by Charles Alban Buckler.

22. Tewkesbury Abbey. Watercolour by W. Buckler, 1845. Additional MS. 37121, no. 29. 26cm × 35.3cm. From the same collection as exhibit 21.

23. Psalter. Arundel MS. 230. Latin and French, late twelfth century, with thirteenth-century additions. Vellum, 194 folios. 26cm × 17.3cm. Written and illuminated probably at Peterborough Abbey, but with a calendar of Crowland Abbey, of the same period as the original part of the manuscript, added at the front.

24. Calendar of Ely Cathedral priory. Harley MS. 547. Latin, thirteenth century. Vellum, 95 folios. 20.5cm × 14.5cm. Gospels and psalter.

25. Ordinal of Bury St Edmunds Abbey. Harley MS. 2977. Latin, fourteenth century. Vellum, 50 folios. 19.6cm × 12.6cm. Incomplete, Advent to the feast of Sts Philip and James Apostles (1st May).

26. Martyrology of St Augustine's Abbey, Canterbury. Cotton MS. Vitellius C. xii. Latin, first quarter of twelfth century and thirteenth century. Vellum, 156 folios. 33cm × 24.2cm. Composite volume. The martyrology belongs to the twelfth-century part and has illuminations, including historiated initials.

27. Offices of Sts Cuthbert, Benedict, and Guthlac. Harley MS. 1117. Latin, *c.*1000. Vellum, 66 folios. 25.5cm × 17.5cm. Breviary supplement, written and illuminated for some monastic church in the west of England, possibly Sherborne.

28. Breviary of Muchelney Abbey, vol. i. Additional MS. 43405. Latin, French, and English, late thirteenth century, with twelfth-to-sixteenth-century additions. Vellum, xxxv + 266 folios. 25.5cm × 16cm. The volume contains the services of the temporale and the rite of blessing holy water. Volume ii of the breviary is Additional MS. 43406.

29. Breviary of Coldingham priory. Harley MS. 4664. Latin, c.1270, with fourteenth-to-fifteenth-century additions. Vellum, 333 folios. 26cm × 18cm. Written and illuminated possibly at Durham Cathedral priory, the mother house of Coldingham. Historiated initials and one miniature. Ex-libris of Richard Crosby, monk of Durham, to whom it was given by Hugh Whitehead, last prior and first dean of Durham, 1521.

30. Cluniac Breviary and Missal. Additional MS. 49363. Latin, c.1300. Vellum, iv + 380 folios. 15cm × 10cm. Written and illuminated possibly for use when travelling, perhaps by a superior of the jurisdiction of La Charité-sur-Loire in England. Historiated initials.

31. Mitre of Wilfrid Upson, first abbot of Prinknash, 1938–1961. Prinknash Abbey, Gloucester. Made at Prinknash in 1938.

32. The Leofric Missal. Oxford, Bodleian Library, MS. Bodley 579. Latin and Anglo-Saxon, early tenth century, with tenth- and eleventh-century additions. Vellum, 377 folios. 20cm × 14cm. Sacramentary, written and illuminated probably in the south-west of England, possibly at Glastonbury Abbey, by a continental scribe. Presumably at Glastonbury c.970, when a Glastonbury calendar and other material were added to it. The illumination in the original part includes decorated initials and borders, a mid-tenth-century addition has one decorated initial, and the additions c.970 have illumination, which includes four miniatures. Belonged to Leofric, bishop of Exeter 1046–1072, by whom it was given to Exeter Cathedral.

33. The Benedictional of St Ethelwold. Additional MS. 49598. Latin, between 963 and 984. Vellum, ii + 119 + 26*, 26** folios (ff. ib and ii are paper laid on vellum). 29.1cm × 21.9cm. Written and illuminated for St Ethelwold, bishop of Winchester 963–984, probably at Winchester. The scribe was a monk called Godeman, probably of Winchester and afterwards abbot of Thorney. The illumination includes twenty-eight full-page miniatures framed by arches or rectangular borders, similar frames on twenty other pages, and two historiated initials.

34. Chasuble. Stanbrook Abbey, Worcester. Twentieth century. White silk, 132cm × 162cm. Hand-woven by the nuns of Stanbrook.

35. The Guthlac Roll. Harley Roll Y. 6. c.1196. Vellum. 16.5cm × 272cm. Outline drawings in medallions of scenes from the life of St Guthlac, made possibly at Crowland Abbey.

36. Rubbing of the sepulchral brass in St Albans Abbey of Thomas de la Mare, abbot of St Albans

1350–1396. Additional MS. 32489. R. 2. Mid-nineteenth century. 300cm × 146cm. From the collection of the Rev. Aeneas Barkly Hutchison.

37. Breviary of St Albans Abbey. Department of Printed Books, C. 110. a. 27. Latin, c.1526. Paper. 14.3cm × 8.5cm. Printed on the layman, John Herford's, press at St Albans.

38. Psalter and Hours. Additional MS. 21927. Latin, twelfth century. Vellum, 116 folios. 26.8cm × 17.4cm. Written possibly at Muchelney Abbey.

39. Book of Hours of the use of Durham Cathedral priory. Harley MS. 1804. Latin, c.1500. Vellum, 138 folios. 14.2cm × 8.2cm.

40. St Albans Abbey, the choir. Watercolour by C.A. Buckler. Additional MS. 37121, no. 19. 36.2cm × 26.1cm.

41. Gradual and Troper of St Albans Abbey. Royal MS. 2 B. iv. Latin, twelfth century. Vellum, 215 folios. 26cm × 16.5cm. Illuminated.

42. Gradual of Crowland Abbey. Egerton MS. 3759. Latin, second quarter of thirteenth century, with fourteenth-century additions. Vellum, vii + 157 folios. 21.8cm × 14.6cm.

43. Missal of the use of Durham Cathedral priory. Harley MS. 5289. Latin, fourteenth century. Vellum, 497 folios. 26.5cm × 17cm. Given to the altar of Sts John the Baptist and Margaret, of the nine altars, at Durham, by John, prior of Durham.

44. Processional of Durham Cathedral priory. Royal MS. 7 A. vi. Latin and English, fourteenth century, with fifteenth-century additions. Vellum, 129 folios. 24.5cm × 16.5cm. Hymns and prayers, chiefly addressed to the Virgin Mary. The processional is one of the additions.

45. Offices for the Sick, the Dying, and the Dead, of the use of Bury St Edmunds Abbey. Harley MS. 5334. Latin, fourteenth century. Vellum, 99 folios. 12.2cm × 7.7cm. Belonged to John Fenyngham, monk of Bury.

46. The Anderson Pontifical. Additional MS. 57337. Latin and Anglo-Saxon, c.1000. Vellum, ii + 144 folios. 30cm × 21.4cm. Pontifical of the Anglo-Saxon tradition, including services for the consecration of a church, ordinations to various offices, the blessing of an abbot, and a coronation order. Some musical notation.

47. *Rituale Abbatum sub regula Sancti Patris Benedicti in congregatione Anglicana.* Stanbrook Abbey, Worcester. Latin, 1963. Paper, 22 pages. 30cm × 22cm. Printed by Stanbrook Abbey Press.

48. The Lindesey Psalter. London, Society of Antiquaries, MS. 59. Latin, 1220–1222. Vellum, v + 256 folios. 24cm × 15cm. Executed for Robert of

Lindesey, abbot of Peterborough 1214–1222, according to an inscription on the fly-leaf: 'Psalterium Roberti de Lindeseye abbatis'. Some prayers, *etc.,* added in the thirteenth or fourteenth century. Two full-page miniatures, tinted drawings, historiated and decorated initials. Fourteenth(?)-century binding of wooden boards covered with white skin.

49. The Sherborne Chartulary. Additional MS. 46487. Latin and Anglo-Saxon, after 1146. Vellum, ii + 88 folios. 27.3cm × 18.2cm. Liturgical texts preceded by copies of charters. Miniatures, decorated initials. Medieval covers of heavy oak boards, the front decorated with a small enamel plaque.

50. St Albans Abbey. Watercolour by J. Buckler, 1832. Additional MS. 37121, no. 18. 27cm × 39.1cm. From the same collection as exhibit 21.

51. Obituary roll of Lucy (de Vere?), foundress and first prioress of Castle Hedingham, Essex. Egerton MS. 2849. Latin, *c.*1230. Vellum, 584cm. × 20cm. Three tinted drawings, circular letter of the prioress Agnes and community of Hedingham, and *tituli* of one hundred and twenty-two religious houses. Decorated initials.

52. Selby Abbey. Watercolour, artist unspecified. Additional MS. 37121, no. 23. 30.7cm × 47.3cm. From the same collection as exhibit 21.

53. St Augustine's Abbey, Canterbury, St Ethelbert's tower. Watercolour by W. A. Buckler. Additional MS. 37120, no. 12. 26.7cm × 20.3cm. From the same collection as exhibit 21.

54. Durham Cathedral priory. Drawing by J. Buckler, 1808. Additional MS. 37120, no. 14. 38.1cm × 31.7cm. From the same collection as exhibit 21.

55. Grant by King Edgar to Ethelwold, bishop of Winchester, of land at Madingley, Cambridgeshire. Harley Charter 43. C. 6. Latin, with boundaries in Anglo-Saxon, 975. Vellum, 25cm × 37.5cm. Witnessed by Dunstan, archbishop of Canterbury, Oswald, archbishop of York, Ethelwold, and others.

56. Two chartularies of Worcester Cathedral priory. Cotton MS. Tiberius A. xiii. Latin and Anglo-Saxon, early eleventh century and 1090–1100. Vellum, 1* + 200 folios. 30.8cm × 22.8cm. Both written at Worcester, the second compiled by the monk Hemming who is identified on f. 131b: 'Ego Hemmingus monachus et sacerdos'. Index of places added in the fifteenth century after the two chartularies had already been bound together.

57. Chartulary of Winchester Cathedral priory. Additional MS. 15350. Latin and Anglo-Saxon, *c.*1130–1150. Vellum, 121 folios. 39cm × 27.6cm. Written at Winchester in bookhand with decorated initials. Medieval binding preserved separately.

58 and 59. Second seal of Norwich Cathedral priory. D.S. lviii. 3 and 4. 1258. Sulphur cast. Diameter 9cm. Obverse and reverse.

60. Grant of land by Prior Peter and the community of Bath Cathedral priory to the abbey of Margam, Glamorganshire. Harley Charter 75. A. 30. Latin, 1159–1166. Vellum, 18cm × 11cm. Pendent seals in red wax of Bath priory and Robert of Lewes, bishop of Bath and Wells.

61. Memorandum-book of Henry of Eastry, prior of Christ Church, Canterbury. Cotton MS. Galba E. iv. Latin, 1285–1331. Vellum, i + 244 folios. 39cm × 29cm. Heading: 'Memoriale multorum Henrici prioris'. Composite volume. Bound with a twelfth-century manuscript of scientific works from Bury St Edmunds Abbey.

62. Appropriation of the church of Edlesborough, Buckinghamshire, by St Albans Abbey, supported by a bull of Pope Urban VI. Additional Charter 19911. Latin, 11th October 1389. Vellum, 54cm × 46.5cm. Seal of Abbot Thomas de la Mare pendent in red wax, backed with uncoloured wax and attached by a plaited cord.

63. Second seal of Christ Church Cathedral priory, Canterbury. D.S. xl. 2. In use from 1175 to the beginning of the fifteenth century. Marbled green wax. Diameter 9cm.

64. Grant of land in Suffolk by Simon of Luton, abbot of Bury St Edmunds to Walter of Luton Additional Charter 7211. Latin, 1257–1279. Vellum, 14.3cm × 20.5cm. Pendent seal of the abbot in bronze-green wax.

65. Bath Abbey. Watercolour by C. A. Buckler. Additional MS. 37120. no. 5. 34cm × 47cm. From the same collection as exhibit 21.

66. The New Minster Liber Vitae. Stowe. MS. 944. Latin and Anglo-Saxon, probably 1031, with additions down to the sixteenth century. Vellum, 69 folios. 25.5cm × 13.5cm. Written at the New Minster, afterwards Hyde, Abbey, Winchester, the original scribe being Aelsine, a monk of the house, whose hand also occurs in exhibits 18 and 19. Two illustrations in tinted outline, belonging to the original part of the book.

67. Liber Vitae of Durham Cathedral priory. Cotton MS. Domitian A. vii. Latin and Anglo-Saxon, mid-ninth century, with additions down to the sixteenth century. Vellum, 84 folios. 21cm × 13.5cm. Originally written at Lindisfarne Cathedral priory, taken with them by the community when they fled before the Vikings in 875, beginning a period of wanderings which include settlement at Chester-le-Street 883–995 and ended with establishment at Durham in 995.

68. The Golden Book of St Albans. Cotton MS. Nero D. vii. Latin, 1380, with additions down to the sixteenth century. Vellum, 1* + 157 folios. 36cm × 23.7cm. Benefactors Book of St Albans Abbey, originally compiled by Thomas Walsingham, monk of St Albans, written out by William de Wyllum monk of St Albans, and illustrated by Alan Strayler, a layman. The additions also have illustrations.

69. Customary of the Shrine of St Thomas Becket. Additional MS. 59616. Latin and French, late thirteenth century and 1428. Vellum, vii + 142 folios. 35cm × 25cm. Two lives of Becket in French, one by Benedict of St Albans, the other by Guernes de Pont-Sainte-Maxence, make up the original part of the book, to which is prefixed the customary in Latin, compiled in 1428 by John Vyel and Edmund Kyngyston, monks of Christ Church Cathedral priory, Canterbury, and at that time guardians of the shrine. The whole manuscript was written at Christ Church, Canterbury.

70. List of relics at Glastonbury Abbey. Cotton MS. Titus D. vii. Latin, fourteenth and fifteenth centuries. Vellum, 163 folios. 15.5cm × 11.3cm. Composite volume. The list belongs to the fourteenth-century material.

71. John Lydgate, monk of Bury St Edmunds, *Life of St Edmund.* Harley MS. 2278. English and Latin, after 1433. Vellum, 119 folios. 25cm × 16.5cm. Written and illuminated at the order of William Curteys, abbot of Bury, as a gift to King Henry VI, who spent Christmas 1433 to 23rd April 1434 at Bury.

72. Pilgrim's sign, showing head and bust of St Thomas Becket. British Museum, Department of Medieval and Later Antiquities, 56, 7–1, 2030. Lead. 9cm × 5cm.

73. Pilgrim's sign, a Canterbury bell. British Museum, Department of Medieval and Later Antiquities, 56, 7–1, 2044. Pewter. 3.5cm × 3.5cm.

74. Pilgrim's sign, gloves of St Thomas Becket. British Museum, Department of Medieval and Later Antiquities, 13, 6–19, 59 and 52, 9–30, 2. Lead. 2.7cm × 2cm and 3cm × 1.5cm.

75. Pilgrim's sign, showing St Thomas Becket on horseback. British Museum, Department of Medieval and Later Antiquities, 56, 7–1, 2035. Lead. 10cm × 8cm.

76. Matrix for casting pilgrim's signs of St Thomas Becket on horseback. British Museum, Department of Medieval and Later Antiquities, 90, 10–2, 1. Honestone slab. 9.5cm × 8.5cm.

77. Pilgrim's sign, showing geese in a pen. British Museum, Department of Medieval and Later Antiquities, 36, 6–10, 73. Lead. 3cm × 4.5cm.

78. Pilgrim's sign, showing a hand holding a bunch of flowers. British Museum, Department of Medieval and Later Antiquities, 71, 7–14, 73. Lead. 4.5cm × 5cm.

79. Pilgrim's sign, showing a pelican in her piety. British Museum, Department of Medieval and Later Antiquities, 04, 7–20, 15. Lead. 5.5cm × 5cm.

80. St Albans Abbey, the interior during a procession. Watercolour by J.C. Buckler. Additional MS. 37122 B, no. 5. 61cm × 43cm. From the same collection as exhibit 21.

81. Pardoner's letter, on behalf of R., prior of King's Mead nunnery, Derby, requesting alms for the rebuilding of the nunnery and rehearsing the indulgences and other spiritual benefits thereby gained. Wolley Charter XI, 25. Latin, after 1216. Vellum. 40cm × 31.2cm.

82. Letter of indulgence from Gilbert Foliot, bishop of Hereford 1147–1163, in favour of pilgrims to the relics of St James the Great at Reading Abbey on his feast-day, or during its octave. Additional Charter 19587. Latin. Vellum, with seal of the bishop. 12.3cm × 17cm.

83. Letter of indulgence from John de Stanford, archbishop of Dublin, in favour of all visiting Reading Abbey and giving alms to it. Additional Charter 19635. Latin, 25th June 1292. Vellum, with seal of the archbishop. 9.5cm × 17.5cm.

84. Malmesbury Abbey. Watercolour by J. Buckler, 1808. Additional MS. 37792, f.5. 46.2cm × 66.3cm.

85. Matthew Paris, monk of St Albans, Map of England and part of Scotland. Cotton MS. Claudius D. vi, f.12b. After 1245 (?). Vellum. 33.6cm × 24.5cm. From a volume compiled in the fourteenth century containing Paris's autograph of the *Abbreviatio Chronicorum* and chronicles, *etc.*, by other authors.

86. Eadmer, monk of Christ Church, Canterbury, *Historia Nouorum in Anglia.* Cotton MS. Titus A. ix. Latin, *c.*1200. Vellum, 130 folios. 21cm × 14cm. Decorated initials.

87. William of Malmesbury, *Gesta Pontificum Anglorum.* Oxford, Magdalen College, MS. 172. Latin, early twelfth century. Vellum, 106 folios. 17.5cm × 12cm. Autograph, with erasures, interlineations and marginal additions. Fourteenth-century shelf-mark of Bury St Edmunds Abbey.

88. Matthew Paris, *Historia Anglorum, etc.* Royal MS. 14 C vii. Latin, 1250–1259, with late-fourteenth-century additions. Vellum, ii + 232 folios. 35.5cm × 24cm. The only complete text of the *Historia Anglorum,* covering the years 1070–1253, followed by an additional section intended for the *Chronica Majora* for the period 1254–1259; both autograph with marginal drawings and shields of arms. An anonymous hand recorded Paris's death in 1259 and continued the chronicle to 1272. Preliminary matter in Paris's hand but unconnected with the texts includes a map of Great Britain, a tinted drawing of the Virgin and Child and imaginary portraits of the kings of England. A note of donation, partly erased, seems to indicate that Matthew Paris gave the volume to St Albans Abbey.

89. John, monk of Glastonbury, Chronicle. Cotton MS. Tiberius A. v. Latin, fifteenth century. Vellum, 164 folios. 22cm × 14cm. An imperfect copy, ending in 1334, of the original version which extended to 1400.

90. Aelfric, monk of the Old Minster, Winchester, and abbot of Eynsham, Homilies (third series). Cotton MS. Julius E. vii. Anglo-Saxon and Latin, early eleventh century. Vellum, 241 folios. 27.5cm × 19cm. Some English interlinear glosses in a sixteenth-century hand. Thirteenth-century ex-libris of Bury St Edmunds Abbey, 'Liber Sancti Aedmundi regis et martyris'.

91. Godfrey, prior of the Old Minster, Winchester, Epigrams. Cotton MS. Vitellius A. xii. Latin, late twelfth century. Vellum, 185 folios. 26.5cm × 22cm. Composite volume.

92. Nigel, monk of Christ Church, Canterbury, *Speculum Stultorum*. Additional MS. 38665. Latin, early fifteenth century. Vellum, 186 folios. 20cm × 13.3cm. The *Speculum Stultorum*, which is preceded by an introductory letter to William Longchamp, Bishop of Ely and is embellished with marginal drawings of asses and monks, forms part of a volume of miscellaneous material. Some other sections of the manuscript are in the hand of John Strecch, Augustinian canon, and relate to that order. Original binding of kid over oak boards.

93. John Lydgate, monk of Bury St Edmunds, Poems. Lansdowne MS. 699. English, fifteen century. Vellum and paper, 176 folios. 19cm × 13.5cm. A collection of Lydgate's works, including *The Lives and Passions of St Alban and St Amphibal*. A note at the head of this poem records the patronage of John Whethamstede, abbot of St Albans.

94. John Lydgate, *The glorious lyfe and passion of seint Albon* ... Department of Printed Books, C. 34. g. 17. English. Paper, unpaginated. 17cm × 11.5cm. Three woodcuts. Printed at St Albans by John Herford, 1534.

95. The Lambeth Bible, vol. i. London, Lambeth Palace Library, MS. 3. Latin, mid twelfth century. Vellum, i + 329 folios. 50.5cm × 40cm. The present volume contains Genesis to Job; volume ii, much mutilated, is MS. P. 5 in the Maidstone Museum,

Kent. Written and illuminated probably for, possibly at, St Augustine's Abbey, Canterbury. The illumination includes six large or full-page miniatures and twenty-four historiated initials in volume i and five historiated initials in volume ii.

96. St Augustine, *De Doctrina Christiana, De Vera Religione, De Poenitentia*. Royal MS. 5 B xii. Latin, late twelfth century. Vellum, i + 166 folios. 26.5cm × 18cm. Decorated initials. A catalogue of the library of Rochester Cathedral priory compiled in 1202 by Alexander, sometime precentor, has been added on the fly-leaves. The present volume is the eleventh item listed. In a contemporary hand on f.4b the Rochester ex-libris, 'Liber de claustro Roffensi' with anathema, and 'Memoriale Humfridi precentoris'.

97. St Augustine, *De Trinitate*. Royal MS. 5 B iv. Latin, twelfth century. Vellum, 182 folios. 29.3cm × 19cm. Thirteenth-century ex-libris of Rochester Cathedral priory, 'Liber de claustro Roffensi' with anathema, and opposite, the name of the scribe: 'Liber beati augustini de Trinitate, quem in eodem claustro scripsit Humfridus precentor'. On the last folio, the *cautio* of John Kyrkby, by whom the volume was pledged in 1468.

98. St Gregory the Great, *Moralia on Job*. Royal MS. 6 C. vi. Latin, early twelfth century. Vellum, 260 folios. 33.5cm × 24cm. Parts iv–vi of the commentary, to which a thirteenth-century hand has prefaced the relevant text. Decorated and historiated initials. Ex-libris of Rochester Cathedral priory and notice of commission or donation by Ralph d'Escures, bishop of Rochester 1108–1114 and archbishop of Canterbury, 'Liber de claustro Roffensi per Radulfum archiepiscopum'.

99. Bestiary and Lapidary. Royal MS. 12 F. xiii. Latin and French, early thirteenth century. Vellum, 152 folios. 30cm × 20.5cm. Illuminated initials and miniatures (incomplete). Ex-libris of Rochester Cathedral priory, with reference to an unidentified donor, 'Liber de claustro Roffensi R. precentoris'.

100. St Augustine, *Enarrationes super Psalmos*. Royal MS. 5 D. ii. Latin, early twelfth century. Vellum, 237 folios. 37cm × 25cm. The third volume of a set, covering psalms ci–cl. Decorated and historiated initials in two distinct styles. Fourteenth-century ex-libris of Rochester Cathedral priory, with notice of commission or donation by Ernulf, bishop of Rochester 1114–1124, 'Tertia pars psalterii Ernulphi episcopi secundum Augustinum, Liber de claustro Roffensi'.

101. Bible. The books of Joshua, Judges, Ruth and Kings in St Jerome's translation. Royal MS. 1 C.vii. Latin, mid-twelfth century. Vellum, vi + 189 folios. 39cm × 27.5cm. Decorated and historiated initials. The style of illumination suggests that this volume was produced at Rochester Cathedral priory.

102. John of Salisbury, *Liber Policraticus*. Royal MS. 12 F. viii. Latin, *c*.1200. Vellum, iii + 115 folios. 29cm × 18.5cm. Decorated initials and marginal drawings. Ex-libris of Rochester Cathedral priory, with notice of commission or donation, 'Liber de claustro Roffensi per Ierardum monachum'. Described in the thirteenth-century catalogue (exhibit 96) as being in the possession of Robert, prior of Walton, the Rochester cell near Felixstowe.

103. Philosophical treatises. Royal MS. 12 D. xiv. Latin, late thirteenth century. Vellum, 157 folios. 26.7cm × 18cm. Translations of the *Metaphysics* and *Ethics* of Aristotle, together with the *Liber de Causis*. Illuminated initials with figures and grotesques. Ex-libris of Rochester Cathedral priory, with notice of commission or donation by John of Shepey, prior of Rochester 1333–1352, 'Liber de claustro Roffensi per magistrum Johannem de Scapeya priorem'. The *cautio* of William of Tunbridge (?) shows that the manuscript was pledged at Oxford in 1321 for 10s.

104. Letter of John Ap Rice to Thomas Cromwell on his visitation of Bury St Edmunds Abbey. Cotton MS. Cleopatra E. iv, f.145. English, 5th November 1535. Paper. 31.2cm × 21.5cm. From a composite volume of papers and letters relating to the Reformation and the Dissolution of the monasteries.

105. Deed of surrender of Athelney Abbey. London, Public Record Office, E 322/8. Latin, 8th February 1539. Vellum. 22.5cm × 48.3cm. Pendent conventual seal in red wax. Attested by seven witnesses in the left-hand margin and signed at the foot by John Tregonwell, the commissioner. From the Court of Augmentations records preserved in the Exchequer.

106. List of manuscripts found in thirty-five Lincolnshire monasteries, compiled by John Leland (?). Royal MS. Appendix 69. English, *c*.1533–1538. Paper, 9 folios. 29.5cm × 18.5cm. In the hand of a contemporary copyist, with autograph annotations by Henry VIII.

107. Extract from a compotus roll of the Court of Augmentations for the sale of the lands and possessions of Ramsey Abbey. Additional Charter 34279. Latin. Paper. 150cm × 31cm. Recites letters patent of Henry VIII dated 4th March 1540, granting the site and appurtenances to Richard Cromwell, nephew of Thomas Cromwell, for £4,963 4s. 2d. and an annual rent of £29 16s.

108. Grant of a pension from the Crown to Thomas Heathe, former monk of Pershore Abbey. Additional Charter 42608. Latin, 12th February 1540. Vellum. 13.5cm × 30cm. A pension of £6 to be paid annually to the grantee until he be promoted to some ecclesiastical benefice, or benefices, of that or greater value. Pendent seal of the Court of Augmentations in uncoloured wax (imperfect). Witnessed by Richard Rich.

109. Thomas Cromwell's Remembrances for the trial and execution of the abbots of Reading and Glastonbury. Cotton MS. Titus B. i, f.441. English, before 27th October 1539. Paper. 31.5cm × 20.5cm. Autograph. From a composite volume of state papers and letters of the reigns of Henry VII and Henry VIII.

110. Whitby, the ruins of the abbey. Watercolour by J. C. Buckler. Additional MS. 37121, no.33. 38.7cm × 31.6cm. From the same collection as exhibit 21.

111. Letters patent of Henry VIII granting to John Hygford of Henwood, Warwickshire, the site and lands of Henwood priory. Additional Charter 44458. Latin, 26th February 1540. Vellum. 45.5cm × 81cm. The Great Seal of England in green wax pendent on a plaited cord. Portrait initial H showing the king enthroned, the headline partly illuminated in gold and embellished with a crown, roses, and fleurs-de-lys. Two attached receipts in English record payment in two instalments of the consideration of £207 5s.

112. Letter from Augustine Baker to Sir Robert Cotton, 3rd June 1629. Cotton MS. Julius C. iii, ff. 12–12b. Paper. 21cm × 16cm.

113. Augustine Baker, *Sancta Sophia*, vol. i, Iohn Patté and Thomas Fievet, Douai, 1657. Department of Printed Books, G. 20024. Octavo. With an engraved portrait.

114. David Knowles, *The Monastic Order in England*, Cambridge, first edition 1940, reprint 1950.

115. Gregory Dix, *The Shape of the Liturgy*, first edition 1945, reprint 1978.

116. Basil Hume, *Searching for God*, 1977.

117. *The Ampleforth Journal*, vol. lxxx, part ii, 1975.

118. *The Douai Magazine*, vol. xxvii, no. 2, 1974.

119. *The Downside Review*, vol. xcv, no. 320, 1977.

120. *Laudate*, Nashdom Abbey, vol. xxix, no. 90, 1951.

121. Letter from Bede Polding, monk of Downside, vicar apostolic of Australia, archbishop of Sydney 1842, to Bishop Thomas Brown, monk of Downside, 27th September, 1838. Downside Abbey, Bath, Archives, K. 104. Paper, 2 folios. 33cm × 41cm.

122. Mortuary bill of St Ambrose Barlow, executed at Lancaster 1641. Downside Abbey, Bath. Paper, 27.5cm × 19cm.

123. Engraving of St Ambrose Barlow. Oxford, Ashmolean Museum, Department of Western Art, C. I, 355, *Clarendon History of the Great Rebellion*, vol. i, p. 355. 8.7cm × 5.8cm.

124. Engraving of the Blessed Philip Powel, executed at Tyburn 1646. Downside Abbey, Bath. 13.5cm × 8.5cm.

125. Bull 'Plantata' of Pope Urban VIII, affirming the continuity of the restored English Benedictine Congregation with the ancient congregation, 12th July 1633. Downside Abbey, Bath. Vellum, 24 folios. 35cm × 24cm. With bulla.

126. Brochure of Douai Abbey and School, Reading. Contemporary.

127. Prospectus of Downside School, *c.*1854. Downside Abbey, Bath, Archives, Box 1411. Paper, 1 folio. 26cm × 21cm.

128. Ceramic altar vessels. Prinknash Abbey, Gloucester. Made by Prinknash, 1979.